THE ST
THE BIBLE

VOLUME I:
THE OLD TESTAMENT

THE STORY OF
THE BIBLE

VOLUME I: *The Old Testament*
Text Book
Test Book
Teacher's Manual
Activity Book
Audio Dramatization
Video Lecture Series

VOLUME II: *The New Testament*
Text Book
Test Book
Teacher's Manual
Activity Book
Audio Dramatization
Video Lecture Series

THE STORY OF
THE BIBLE

VOLUME I:
THE OLD TESTAMENT

TAN

The Story of the Bible: Volume I, The Old Testament © 2015 TAN Books, PO Box 410487, Charlotte, NC 28241.

Most of the content of this book originally appeared in *Bible History: A Textbook of the Old and New Testaments for Catholic Schools* © 1931 Benziger Brothers, Inc., Printer to the Holy Apostolic See, New York. The rights were purchased from Benziger by TAN Books in 2000.

Nihil obstat for *Bible History*: Arthur J. Scanlan, S.T.D.

Imprimatur for *Bible History*: + Patrick Cardinal Hayes
Archbishop of New York
New York City, New York
July 1, 1931

The Story of the Bible: Volume I, The Old Testament includes an extensively revised and updated version of the Old Testament portion of *Bible History*, edited by Brian Kennelly and Paul Thigpen, Ph.D.

Scripture quotations are from the Revised Standard Version of the Bible—Second Catholic Edition (Ignatius Edition). Copyright © 2006, Division of Christian Education of the National Council of the Churches of Christ in the United States of America. Used by permission. All rights reserved.

Cover and illustrations by Chris Pelicano

Maps by Abby Glazier

ISBN: 978-1-61890-644-1

Cataloging-in-Publication data on file with the Library of Congress

Printed and bound in the United States of America
TAN Books
www.TANBooks.com
Charlotte, North Carolina
2015

CONTENTS

O sing to the Lord a new song,
for he has done marvelous things!
His right hand and his holy arm
    have gotten him victory.

The Lord has made known his victory,
    he has revealed his vindication in the sight of the nations.

He has remembered his steadfast love and faithfulness
    to the house of Israel.

—Psalm 98 (1–3a)

THE OLD TESTAMENT

The Story of the Bible will take you through the adventures of both Testaments, in two volumes. This first volume covers the Old Testament, and the second volume covers the New Testament.

INTRODUCTION

Your Time Has Come

Get ready for an adventure.

Open your mind and stretch your imagination. Soon we'll travel back in time to trace the origins of the universe and of the human race. Through the power of a Book unlike any other book, we can journey to a distant age, all the way back to the first age.

By the time this voyage is complete, you'll arrive back home in the present day. But what you learn along the way will help you understand better your unique place in today's world. And it will allow you to look forward, with hope and wonder, to the world to come.

Your ancestors before you, those who lived in the days of old, once sat by firelight as they studied and learned from this Book. It's filled with tales of adventure, betrayal, vengeance, war, love, heroism, and hope. As you embark on this journey, you'll come to know men and women of great holiness, and some of great wickedness as well. You'll encounter angels and demons, kings and queens, warriors and prophets—and everyday people like yourself, all with a story to tell.

Your time has come to learn this story. *It's your turn now.* You must take this Book, the one we call the Bible, and learn everything there is to know about it. Think of it as a flaming torch that has been carried through the long, dark nights of human history, a torch that has now been passed to you. Take it, steady it, and move forward with its knowledge and wisdom, so that one day you can pass it on to the ones who follow you.

But before you take up this torch, burning with the power of God's Word, it's important to understand why our heavenly Father gave it to us.

The Book of Nature

God created us to know Him, love Him, and serve Him in this world, so that we can be happy with Him forever in the world to come. The better we know Him, the more we'll love Him; and the more we love Him, the more eager we'll be to do His holy will.

For this reason, the most important lessons we must learn are those that help us to know more and more about God.

We can learn many things about God from the world around us. The radiant stars, moon, and sun that light the sky; the fragrant forests and pastures, dotted with blossoms; the towering mountains and vast deserts—all these were made by God. They are *beautiful*, so they tell us that the God who made them is *beautiful*.

The mighty rivers flow, and the great waterfalls come crashing down. The ocean tides rise and fall, and no one can resist them. Storms come thundering with lightning and gale winds. All these are *powerful*, so they tell us that the God who made them is *powerful*.

Our families and friends are kind and good to us. They watch over us lovingly and take care of our needs. So they show us that the God who made them is *loving and caring*.

In all these ways, the world tells us about our God. Since He's the One who created it, we might think of Him as an Author, and the world as His Book. Just as an author writes words on a page, so God writes with his divine Hand on the sky, the land, the sea, and the people of our world. Each morning when we open our eyes, we're able to read from this "Book of Nature" that He's written.

Even so, we need more than this "book" all around us to understand who God is and how He wants us to live. That's because we aren't always able to read correctly the wonderful lessons that are found in the Book of Nature. The things of this world are so beautiful and powerful and good that we may be tempted to think more of them than we do of the God who made them. We may end up loving them more than we love God.

But there's another reason as well why we need more than the Book of Nature to learn about God. We find that many important things about God and His will for us aren't written in that book. Some truths are above and beyond nature, and we call these *supernatural*.

God knows these truths because He is all-wise and knows all things. He wants to share them with us. Why? If we learn these supernatural truths, we'll know how to love and serve Him in a nobler way. And that will make us far happier than we could ever be if we had to depend on the Book of Nature alone.

Why We Have the Bible
For this reason, God gave us another book, which we call the Bible. It helps us make sense of the lessons that are written in the Book of Nature, as well as many other

things that otherwise we could never know or understand about God, ourselves, and the world around us.

Children can't understand everything that adults can, but even the wisest adult can never understand certain things in the mind of God. They are simply too far beyond us, too complex, too vast, for us to grasp. So we must trust in Him when He tells us that something is true.

How can we trust that everything God says is true? Because He knows all things, and He cannot lie. The truths that we can't fully understand, even after God has told them to us, we call *mysteries*.

The Bible was written by men who were chosen by God especially for that purpose. These men wrote down what God wanted them to write, and nothing else. He guided them so they would not make a mistake. He brought to their memories the truths they had learned, and He placed thoughts in their minds that would never have come to them otherwise. The help that God gave to these sacred writers we call *divine inspiration*.

After Christ ascended into heaven, God inspired some of His apostles and disciples to write down many of the things He had said and done. God watched over them and guided them, making sure they would write all that He wanted them to write. After the generation of the apostles, no one ever had that special gift of divine inspiration again. By that time, God had revealed to us all the truths that are necessary for us to enter into the kingdom of heaven and to live with Him forever.

The Church that Christ founded guards the truths that He revealed. It's like a castle built to protect a great spring of life-giving water. When the spring is protected, the living water can flow out from it to all those who come to drink.

Christ promised to be with His Church—the King in His castle—until the end of time. Through this promise, we know that the Church cannot make a mistake when she tells us what we must believe and do if we wish to know, love, and serve God, both in this life and the next. Because the Church cannot make a mistake in these matters, we say she is *infallible*.

The Parts of the Bible

The Bible is divided into two parts: the *Old Testament* and the *New Testament*. The word "testament" means an agreement, or more exactly, a *covenant*. When two persons enter into a covenant, they promise to give themselves to each other in love and to be faithful in that love. Marriage is one clear example of what we mean by a covenant.

The forty-six books of the Old Testament tell us about the covenant between God and His people before Jesus came into the world. The Old Testament shows us again and again how God loved His covenant people faithfully, even when they broke the covenant and failed to love Him in return. These books tell how God promised us a Redeemer who would save us from our sins, and how He chose a certain nation, the Jews, to prepare the world for the Redeemer's coming.

The New Testament contains twenty-seven books. It tells how God's promise was fulfilled in Our Lord and Savior, Jesus Christ, and in the Church that He founded.

The Bible, then, is one large book, made up of seventy-three smaller ones.

The books in the Bible are not all alike. Some tell the story of things that happened in the past, called historical books. Others contain rules of conduct for how to live properly, called moral books. Others foretell things that will happen in the future, called prophetic books. Some of the books are even written in poetry rather than prose.

The Story of the Bible will take you through the adventures of both Testaments, in two volumes. This first volume covers the Old Testament, and the second volume covers the New Testament.

Scripture and Tradition

We should note one last thing about the truths God has revealed. Even though *Sacred Scripture*—another name for the Bible—is essential for knowing about God, other truths that He wanted us to know were not written down there. Instead, they have come to us by word of mouth and by example, beginning with the preaching and practice of the apostles. Since the time of Jesus, each generation has received these truths and handed them down to the next generation. We call this the *Sacred Tradition*.

We shouldn't be surprised that the Bible can't contain the entire teaching of the Sacred Tradition. Think only, for example, of the life of Our Lord, so full of wonderful teachings and deeds. In the Gospels, we read about many events from Jesus' life. But at the end of the Gospel of John, we're told that there were many other things Jesus said and did. If they all were written down, St. John insists, the whole world couldn't hold the books that would have to be written!

PART ONE
How God Came to Promise Us a Redeemer

CHAPTER 1

In the Beginning

The Story of Creation

From all eternity—before time began—God existed. He always was, and He never had a beginning, just as He will never have an end. He is beyond time, just as the sun is beyond the earth. But just as the sun's rays can enter our world, so God can enter our world ruled by time, while still remaining outside it.

God is infinitely perfect. There is nothing lacking in Him. He needs nothing. The three Divine Persons—the Father, the Son, and the Holy Spirit—are together one God, equal to one another in all things. They possess within themselves everything that's necessary to be eternally happy.

All that is true, all that is beautiful, all that is powerful, and all that is good, is found in God. He doesn't have to look to anyone outside Himself for anything whatsoever. There is no truth that He doesn't know, no power that He doesn't possess, no happiness that He doesn't enjoy. He doesn't need anything or anyone besides Himself.

Because God is good, He wanted others to share in His happiness. That's why He created heaven and earth. He made them out of nothing, not because He needed them, but so that creatures could share in His happiness and glory.

Among the creatures that can have a share in God's happiness and glory are the *angels*. They are like God in that they have no physical body; they are pure spirit. Also like God, they have an *intellect* (the ability to think) and a *free will* (the ability to choose). Not all the angels are alike. It was God's will that some of them be closer to Him than others.

The Bible speaks of nine different ranks of angelic spirits, called *choirs*. There are angels, archangels, principalities, virtues, powers, dominions, thrones, cherubim, and seraphim. According to ancient tradition, the highest ranks of all these are the cherubim and seraphim, while the lowest are angels and archangels.

Yet even though the angels are considered the lowest class of angelic spirits, they are still vital to God's plan. He sends them on missions in our world. Among other roles, they are assigned to watch over human beings and protect them. These protectors are known as our *guardian angels*.

When God created the angels, they had a choice to make. If they were to enjoy the happiness of heaven, they had to love God more than they loved themselves. But God didn't force the angels to love Him. Because they had free will, they could choose to be God's friends or His enemies.

Some of the angels proudly refused to obey God and love Him more than they loved themselves. Because of their pride, they turned against God. The leader of these rebel angels was Lucifer, one of the highest angels that God had created.

God didn't spare the angels who had sinned. The Bible tells of a great battle in heaven. The archangel called Michael led the good angels to fight the bad angels, casting them out of heaven through the power God had given them. From that point on, Lucifer was known as Satan, or the Devil.

The good angels remain in the presence of God. For all eternity they will see Him face to face. They will love and praise Him, and be happy with Him forever. But the fallen angels, whom we also call *demons*, will never see God. All hope of ever entering the kingdom of heaven was lost forever for those who rebelled against Him.

What happened to the angels is a lesson for us all. Just as God gave them free will, He has given us free will. And just as some of the angels used that free will to turn against God, we too have the ability to make such a choice. As we'll see, that's exactly what happened with the first parents of the whole human race. To know their story, and how the human race began, we now turn to the very first book of the Bible.

The Book of Genesis
The first book of the Old Testament, called Genesis, tells us how God made the world. It divides up the whole work of His creation into six days. However, the word "day,"

as used in the Bible, does not necessarily mean a period of twenty-four hours. Each of the "days" of creation may have been a long, long time.

In a similar way, we sometimes say that something happened in George Washington's day, meaning the time period in which he lived. Or we may say that the day of people traveling in horse-drawn wagons has passed, meaning that no one travels that way any longer. In these instances, the word "day" takes on a different meaning from the one we're used to, just as it does in the first part of the Book of Genesis.

We must bear in mind that God didn't inspire the author of the Book of Genesis to tell us exactly how the world was made, how each canyon was dug and each mountain was raised. His purpose was to teach all people, everywhere and until the end of time, that all things were made by God, and without Him, there would be nothing.

Genesis tells the creation story much like a poem, with beautiful images revealing powerful truths when we think about them carefully. We'll quote the whole story here from the pages of the Bible so that you can ponder its meaning:

"In the beginning God created the heavens and the earth. The earth was without form and void, and darkness was upon the face of the deep; and the Spirit of God was moving over the face of the waters. And God said, 'Let there be light'; and there was light. And God saw that the light was good; and God separated the light from the darkness. God called the light Day, and the darkness He called Night. And there was evening and there was morning, one day.

"And God said, 'Let there be a firmament in the midst of the waters, and let it separate the waters from the waters.'

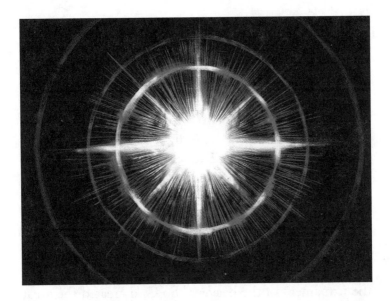

And God made the firmament and separated the waters which were under the firmament from the waters which were above the firmament. And it was so. And God called the firmament heaven. And there was evening and there was morning, a second day.

"And God said, 'Let the waters under the heavens be gathered together into one place, and let the dry land appear.' And it was so. God called the dry land Earth, and the waters that were gathered together He called Seas. And God saw that it was good.

"And God said, 'Let the earth put forth vegetation, plants yielding seed, and fruit trees bearing fruit in which is their seed, each according to its kind, upon the earth.' And it was so. The earth brought forth vegetation, plants yielding seed according to their own kinds, and trees bearing fruit in which is their seed, each according to its kind. And God saw that it was good. And there was evening and there was morning, a third day.

"And God said, 'Let there be lights in the firmament of the heavens to separate the day from the night; and let them be for signs and for seasons and for days and years, and let them be lights in the firmaments of the heavens to give light upon the earth.' And it was so.

"And God made the two great lights, the greater light to rule the day, and the lesser light to rule the night; He made the stars also. And God set them in the firmament of the heavens to give light upon the earth, to rule over the day and over the night, and to separate the light from the darkness. And God saw that it was good. And there was evening and there was morning, a fourth day.

"And God said, 'Let the waters bring forth swarms of living creatures, and let birds fly above the earth across the firmament of the heavens.' So God created the great sea monsters and every living creature that moves, with which the waters swarm, according to their kinds, and every winged bird according to its kind. And God saw that it was good.

"And God blessed them, saying, 'Be fruitful and multiply and fill the waters in the seas, and let birds multiply on the earth.' And there was evening and there was morning, a fifth day.

"And God said, 'Let the earth bring forth living creatures according to their kinds: cattle and creeping things and beasts of the earth according to their kinds.' And it was so. And God made the beasts of the earth according to their kinds and the cattle according to their kinds, and everything that creeps upon the ground according to its kind. And God saw that it was good.

"Then God said, 'Let us make man in our image, after our likeness; and let them have dominion over the fish of the sea, and over the birds of the air, and over the cattle, and over all the earth, and over every creeping thing that creeps upon the earth.' So God created man in His image, in the image of God He created them; male and female He created them.

"And God blessed them, and God said to them, 'Be fruitful and multiply, and fill the earth and subdue it; and have dominion over the fish of the sea and over the birds of the air and over every living thing that moves upon the earth.'

"And God said, 'Behold, I have given you every plant yielding seed which is upon the face of all the earth, and every tree with seed in its fruit; you shall have them for food. And to every beast of the earth, and to every bird of the air, and to everything that creeps on the earth, everything that has the breath of life, I have given every green plant for food.' And it was so.

"And God saw everything that He had made, and behold, it was very good. And there was evening and there was morning, a sixth day.

"Thus the heavens and the earth were finished, and all the host of them. And on the seventh day God finished His work which He had done, and He rested on the seventh day from all His work which He had done. So God blessed the seventh day and hallowed it, because on it God rested from all His work which He had done in creation. These are the generations of the heavens and the earth when they were created." This seventh day came to be called the *Sabbath*.

After this story, Genesis tells us more about how God made human beings in His own image and likeness. We read that He made the first man from the dust of the earth, and breathed into him the breath of life. In this way, the first man became a living being, someone who was like God because he could think and choose and love, just as God does.

Like the angels, however, the man would face the most important choice of all: Would he obey God—or disobey Him?

The Garden of Eden and the Fall of Our First Parents
God called the first man *Adam,* which can mean either "the man" or "made from the earth." He made a wonderful garden called Eden and gave it to Adam as his home. In this garden there were many kinds of trees, all of them beautiful and pleasing to the eye. Each of these trees grew delicious fruit.

The tree of life stood in the middle of Eden, as well as the tree of the knowledge of good and evil. God said to Adam, "You may freely eat of every tree of the garden; but of the tree of the knowledge of good and evil you shall not eat, for in the day that you eat of it you shall die."

Then God brought to Adam all the beasts of the earth and the birds of the air, so that he could give them a name. And Adam called all the animals by their names.

But of all the animals of the earth, not one was worthy to be Adam's companion. He needed someone like himself. So God said, "It is not good that the man should be alone; I will make him a helper fit for him."

Then God sent Adam into a deep sleep, and while he slept, God took one of his ribs and made a woman from it. When Adam awoke, God brought her to him.

"This at last is bone of my bones and flesh of my flesh," Adam said; "she shall be called Woman, because she was taken out of Man." This is why, ever since then, a man leaves his father and mother to join himself to a wife; and the husband and wife become one, a new family. Adam called his wife *Eve,* which means "mother of all living."

When God created Adam and Eve, He gave wonderful gifts to their souls. He clothed their minds and hearts with a grace that would make them holy and pleasing in His sight. They received the ability to know, love, and serve Him for all eternity.

Adam and Eve were very happy together in Eden. Everything around them was beautiful, and there was plenty of food of every kind. A beautiful river flowed through the middle of the garden, between the trees. Adam and Eve loved to walk through the garden, talking to each other and to God.

God told them that they and their children would always be happy if they would love Him with all their hearts and obey Him. They would never die, and they would live with Him forever.

While all this was happening, the powerful angel called Satan was watching. Since he had been cast out of heaven after the great battle of angels, he envied Adam and Eve for their relationship with God. He saw how happy they were in Eden, and how much God loved them. Satan made up his mind to try to lead Adam and Eve away from God.

One day he appeared to Eve in the form of a serpent. He spoke to Eve and asked her whether God had commanded her not to eat from any trees in the garden. Eve explained that they could eat the fruit from many trees in the garden, but they were to stay away from just one tree: the tree of the knowledge of good and evil. If they didn't, they would die.

"You will not die," replied the serpent. "For God knows that when you eat of it your eyes will be opened, and you will be like God, knowing good and evil."

The serpent was trying to trick Eve, tempting her to think she could be like God by disobeying Him. When she heard these words, she forgot how happy she had been in Eden and how good God had been to her. The

fruit from the forbidden tree was beautiful to look at; she gazed on it as the serpent's words echoed in her mind.

Eve wondered how wise she could become if she ate the fruit. So she took some from the tree, ate it, and brought some to Adam. She told him the strange story of the serpent, and then he too ate of the fruit.

It didn't take long for them both to realize what they had done, and how wrong it was to disobey God. They were ashamed and afraid, so they tried to hide from Him. But no one can hide from God.

The Lord found them and asked Adam, "Have you eaten of the tree of which I commanded you not to eat?"

Adam answered by trying to blame Eve for what he had done, since she had brought him the fruit. Then Eve tried to pass the blame on to the serpent, insisting that it had tricked her. But just as they couldn't hide from God, they couldn't run away from what they had done. God knew exactly what had happened.

A Punishment and a Promise
Next, God said to the serpent: "Because you have done this, cursed are you above all cattle, and above all wild animals; upon your belly you shall go, and dust you shall eat all the days of your life. I will put enmity between you and the woman, and between your seed and her seed; he shall bruise your head, and you shall bruise his heel."

The last warning that God delivered to the serpent was the first promise of the Redeemer who would one day come. Much of what God said that day wouldn't make sense until thousands of years later.

After turning from the serpent, God told Eve that He would multiply her pain in giving birth to children, and her husband would rule over her. Then he rebuked Adam for accepting his wife's invitation to eat the forbidden fruit. Since Adam had gone against what God commanded, God told him that from then on, his labors would be difficult as he tried to provide food for his wife and himself.

In the end, they would both die, and their bodies would return to the soil from which they were made. "You are dust," God said, "and to dust you shall return."

Then God clothed Adam and Eve with clothing made from animal skins and cast them out of the Garden of Eden. To the east of the garden He stationed angels called cherubim, along with a flaming sword to guard the way to the tree of life. He made it so they could never return to the garden they once called home.

Adam and Eve had believed the Devil when he lied to them, saying that if they disobeyed God and ate the forbidden fruit, they would become as wise and knowing as God Himself. They had trusted Lucifer and their own desires instead of trusting God, and in doing so, they committed a great sin. So they destroyed their friendship with God, and heaven was closed to them.

We call their sin *original sin*. Because of it, Adam and Eve were no longer happy, their minds were disturbed, and their wills were weakened. Even their bodies were affected; they could suffer from illness and disease.

It became hard for them to know what was true and to do what was right. By their disobedience, their bodies and souls became disordered. They lost the *original righteousness,* the right ordering, that God had given them at their creation.

As a result, when they later had children, Adam and Eve couldn't pass on to them what they themselves no longer possessed. Their children and their children's children, until the end of the world, would lack original righteousness. All the human race to come would suffer for their sin.

Every child, then, is conceived with the stain of original sin on his soul. The only exceptions are our Lord Jesus Christ, who is the sinless Son of God; and His mother, the Blessed Virgin Mary, who was preserved from sin.

CHAPTER 2

The Descendants of Adam and Eve

Cain and Abel

God warned Adam and Eve that life would become difficult as a result of their sin, and they would have to work hard to obtain food and other necessities. They both found this to be true in the days after they left the Garden of Eden.

Eventually they had children, and they told their children the story of their happiness in Eden. They explained how their happiness had been lost through their sin, and that they were very sorry they had disobeyed God.

Yet they didn't lose courage or hope. God had cursed the serpent and promised that a descendant of Eve would crush his head. They told their children that, some day, God would save them from the effects of their sin.

Adam and Eve had many children. The two oldest were named Cain and Abel. Cain was a farmer, growing and gathering the fruits of the fields, trees, and vines. Abel was a shepherd, leading his sheep over the plains in search of pastures and streams. These gifts of the earth came to them from God.

Adam and Eve taught their children how to worship God by offering up to Him some of His gifts as a way of saying thank you. They burned up the gifts so they could never be given to anyone except to God. Such an offering we call a *sacrifice*. It tells God that we want to honor Him as our Creator, and that we know we belong to Him and depend on Him for all we have.

One day, Cain and Abel offered sacrifices to God. Cain offered the fruits of the fields, while Abel placed on his altar some young lambs from his flocks. God was pleased with Abel's sacrifice. But with Cain's, He was displeased, because Cain did not give his gift with a pure heart. Perhaps Cain really wanted to keep the gift and felt resentment toward God.

In any case, God rebuked Cain and pointed out to him that his heart was wrong. But instead of being sorry, Cain grew angry with God and was jealous of Abel. His jealousy was so strong that he ended up hating his brother, and at last he made up his mind to kill him.

Cain began his devious plan by inviting Abel to take a walk out into the fields where Cain worked. Abel agreed; perhaps he felt sorry for Cain and hoped to comfort him. When they were far away and no one could see them, Cain killed Abel, leaving his brother's blood to stain the earth.

Then Cain heard the voice of God asking where his brother was.

Cain responded to God, "I do not know; am I my brother's keeper?"

"What have you done?" God asked. "The voice of your brother's blood is crying to me from the ground."

God knew that Abel's blood had been spilled on the earth by the hands of Cain. He told the murderer that he would now be banned from the soil that had been stained by Abel's blood. The ground would no longer yield to him its fruits when he tried to farm it. From that point on, Cain would have to wander the earth as an exile.

Cain was filled with terror, pleading that he could not bear such a punishment. He feared that because of what he had done, others would want to kill him. But God told him not to fear them. He warned that anyone who killed Cain would suffer a much worse fate.

Then God put a mark on Cain. It made sure that anyone who found him would know not to kill him, but rather should let him wander the earth. And this is what Cain did, wandering the earth in exile, turning away from the presence of the Lord.

The sad story of Cain and Abel shows us how the disobedience of Adam and Eve was to have a tragic and lasting effect on the new human race. The sin of the parents set the pattern for the sins of the children.

Notice how, when dealing with Cain, God asked a question that gave him a chance to admit his guilt. He had done the same with Adam and Eve. But in both cases, instead of confessing their sin and asking forgiveness, they tried to avoid blame and hide what they had done. And in both cases, their efforts failed: God always knows what we've done and what's in our hearts.

In the stories to come, we'll see how the weakness and misery of original sin came to spread throughout the whole world.

Noah, His Ark, and the Great Flood
Adam and Eve had many children, grandchildren, and great-grandchildren, and soon the human family became quite large. Sadly, many of the descendants of Adam and Eve were disobedient, selfish, and wicked. There were some good people, but they married the wicked ones, and in time they too were drawn into sin. They no longer served God and soon forgot Him. Their hearts had become hardened and filled with darkness.

Still, there were a few who believed in God and tried to serve Him. Among these was a good and holy man called Noah. God gave him three sons: Shem, Ham, and Japheth. All three grew up to be good men like their father. They were obedient and did their best to love and serve God.

When God saw how corrupt, violent, and sinful the people had become, He warned Noah that He planned to wipe out their wickedness with a great flood. God said He would send rain for days and days, and the sun would be darkened by violent storm clouds.

Because Noah and his family were faithful and pleasing to God, He intended to spare them. He told Noah to make a large ark, or houseboat. It would be four hundred and fifty feet long, seventy-five feet wide, and forty-five feet high.

A boat of these dimensions would be as long as two city blocks, as wide as four houses, and as high as a five-story building. This massive ark had three levels, with a window and a door. It was covered with a roof, and the entire ship was covered with tar to keep the water out.

When everything was finished, at God's command, Noah began to fill the ark. He brought inside males and females of every kind of animal so they could form animal families. He also brought inside enough food to feed them all. Then at last, Noah took his family into the ark.

Can you imagine how the wicked people laughed at Noah for building such a large ship and filling it with so many animals? They must have thought he had gone crazy. But then the rain began. For forty days and forty nights it rained and rained as it had never rained before.

Soon, the rivers and seas overflowed their boundaries. Human beings and animals must have panicked and tried to find a refuge from the flood. But no matter how high they climbed, there was no place of safety. The water rose higher and higher as the rain continued to pour down from the dark sky, until at last it stood twenty feet above even the highest mountain.

Every living thing left on the land was drowned in the flood. But the ark floated safely across the raging waters. So Noah, his family, and the animals in the ark were saved.

After several weeks, the rain finally stopped and the skies opened up. In the five months following, the ark continued to float around on the water. One day, it came to rest on a mountain.

At first, Noah could see nothing from the window except water. But after a time he saw the tops of some mountains. It was a sign that the water level was going down.

He waited forty days longer and then sent out a raven and a dove. The dove returned because it could not find a place to rest.

A week later he sent forth a second dove. This time the dove returned, carrying an olive branch in its beak. This meant that plants had begun to grow again on the land.

After another week, he sent the dove out a third time. This time, it did not return. Noah knew then that the flood was over.

Seven more weeks passed, and God spoke to Noah. He told him to come out of the ark, along with his family and all the animals. It was time for them all to make new homes. Then they could have new families so that the world could be filled again with creatures of every kind.

Noah left the ark, grateful to God for having saved him and his family from the flood. He built an altar to God and offered on it several animals and birds. God was pleased with the sacrifice of Noah, and promised He would never again destroy the earth by the waters of a flood. God set a rainbow in the sky as a sign of the promise He had made to reward the faithfulness of Noah.

God blessed Noah and his sons and told them that the earth, with all that it contained, was theirs. They began to farm the soil and plant vineyards, living as they had before they entered the ark.

Ham's Sin

Noah and his children made wine from the grapes of the vineyard. One day, Noah drank too much of it. He became drunk and fell asleep on the ground.

When Ham saw his father overcome by wine and sleeping on the ground, he called his brothers and made fun of the old man. But the other brothers were upset by Ham's conduct. They covered their father with a cloak, for they loved him dearly and didn't want to see him treated with disrespect.

When Noah awoke and heard what had happened, he was angry and rebuked Ham. Noah told him that his son, Canaan, would always be the servant of his brothers. But he gave his blessing to Shem and Japheth for the love and respect they had shown him.

Noah went on to live many years after the flood, and he was a very old man when he died. His three sons went on to have many descendants who spread out to distant lands. Yet sadly enough, the sin of Adam and Eve continued to have miserable effects even on the new families that filled the earth.

The Tower of Babel and the Growth of Nations
As the human race grew larger and larger, the descendants of the sons of Noah were in need of richer fields and larger pastures. They moved to the fields of a land called Shinar to settle. There, they made plans to build a city with a tower so high it would reach past the clouds, all the way to the gates of heaven. If they created such an awesome tower, they could become famous and well respected by the whole world.

So the people of Shinar began to build the city and the tower. They baked bricks, then hauled them higher and higher as the tower grew from day to day. From faraway lands, the tower could be seen piercing the sky.

But God could see more than their giant tower. He looked past the grand structure they were building to something much smaller: the heart of each of those who were building it. He saw in their hearts the truth. He knew that they were proud and worked only for their own selfish glory, so He knew He had to stop their project.

One day, while they were working on the tower, the people noticed something very strange. Even though they

normally all spoke the same language, they suddenly couldn't understand one another as they spoke. The language of some became different from the language of others.

They could no longer make sense of what everyone was saying. So they could no longer work together. They stopped building the city and the tower.

The city and tower came to be called *Babel*, which means "confusion." When the one language everyone used became many languages instead, the people were left confused. So the families separated, abandoning the tower of Babel. The Lord scattered them into all the lands.

Several of the lands where great nations eventually formed are of special importance to Bible history.

The valley of the Nile in northeastern Africa was very fertile. The people who settled there had an abundance of food. In time they built great cities, which controlled the small villages and countryside around them. Over a period of centuries, two kingdoms were formed: one in the north, and the other in the south. In the end, these two kingdoms were united under one king, called a *pharaoh*. His kingdom was called Egypt.

Back in Shinar as well, great cities were built. Two rivers flow through this land: the Tigris and the Euphrates. For this reason, it came to be called *Mesopotamia*, which means "land between the rivers." Today that area includes the nation of Iraq and parts of neighboring nations.

A series of powerful kingdoms arose within Mesopotamia. Among them were the Sumerian, Akkadian, Babylonian, and Assyrian kingdoms. Some of these became empires by conquering other nations and peoples.

Finally, we should note some of the peoples who lived in Canaan—the land where God's chosen people, the descendants of Abraham, eventually came to settle. In this area between the Mediterranean Sea and the Jordan River, different peoples known as Chaldeans, Hittites, Philistines, and others made their home. We'll hear much more about all these nations and peoples in the stories to come.

PART TWO

CHAPTER 3

Abraham and Isaac

Abraham, the Father of the Chosen People

Many, many years after the human race had been scattered from Babel, there lived in Ur, a city of the Chaldeans, a herdsman named Terah. This herdsman had three sons, one of whom was named Abram. Abram grew up and married a woman named Sarai. They had no children, but they cared for Abram's nephew, Lot, whose father had died young.

Before Abram's father died, he moved the family from Ur to the city of Haran. After the father's death, God told Abram to leave his native land and go into the land He would show him. Even though Abram and Sarai had no children, God promised to make Abram the father of a great nation.

In him, God said, all the families of the earth would be blessed. So in obedience to God's command, Abram took Sarai, Lot, and all their servants and flocks, and journeyed southwest toward the land of Canaan.

Abram lived the life of a nomad chief. He most likely wore a long robe and a turban atop his head. His home would have been a humble tent with a peaked roof, divided by a curtain of skins into a living room and sleeping room.

His servants, several hundred herdsmen with their wives and children, would have lived in similar tents near their master's. Their food consisted of butter, milk, herbs, bread, the meat of their flocks, and the fruits of the trees.

In his wanderings, Abram came to a city in Canaan called Shechem. As he peered out over the land, God promised this territory to all Abram's children. Abram built an altar to God at Shechem. Next, he pitched his tent at Bethel, where he also built an altar.

The time came when the land of Canaan suffered a great famine. In order to escape it, Abram took his family, which still included Lot, and went south into Egypt. When the famine was over, he returned and settled near Bethel.

Abram and Lot now had many sheep, cattle, and camels. There was not enough pasture land to provide food for them all. Quarrels arose between the herdsmen of Abram and the herdsmen of Lot. Each group wanted the best pasture for their flocks.

Abram didn't want a fight between family members. So he invited Lot to choose which portion of the land he wanted his people to occupy. Then Abram would take the portion that was left.

Lot looked eastward. He chose the country around the Jordan near the cities of Sodom and Gomorrah. He himself dwelt in Sodom, separating himself from Abram.

After Lot had departed, God ordered Abram to lift his eyes and gaze around, from the north to the south, and the east to the west. God said that He would give these lands to Abram and his children forever. Then he promised again that Abram would one day have many descendants.

Abram moved his tent to the valley of Mamre and lived there in the hill country. There he built an altar to God, just as he had done in other lands.

One day a neighboring king came with his allies to plunder the Canaanites. He took many cities, and finally captured Sodom, where Lot lived. The king took the people of Sodom away and made them slaves, including Lot and his household, who were among the captives.

When Abram heard what had happened to his nephew, he gathered together his own men, who numbered three hundred and eighteen. They formed a military alliance with their neighbors. Overtaking the king's army at Damascus, they attacked them and rescued Lot and all his people.

When Abram was returning from the battle, Melchizedek, king of Salem, came forward to meet him with bread and wine. Salem was an important town in the land of Canaan, which later would become the great city of Jerusalem. As was often the case in those days, the king of this small city-state was also a priest.

Melchizedek blessed Abram in the name of the Most High God. Abram offered him a tenth of all his possessions as a token of gratitude for the blessing. Because the priest-king Melchizedek offered a sacrifice of bread and wine, he is an image of Jesus Christ, our King and High Priest, whose sacrifice comes to us in the Eucharist when the bread and wine become His Body and Blood.

Later, God appeared to Abram in a vision and told him not to be afraid. "I am your shield," God said; "your reward shall be very great."

Abram asked what kind of reward would be given to him. He reminded the Lord that he and Sarai had never been blessed with a child. Abram worried that a slave born in his house would have to become his heir. But God put his fears to rest.

He took Abram outside and said, "Look toward heaven, and number the stars, if you are able to number them. . . . So shall your descendants be."

Abram believed God's promise, and his faith pleased

God. But Abram and Sarai continued to grow older, and they still had no children.

Sarai had an Egyptian servant maid named Hagar. Sarai advised Abram to take Hagar as his wife, hoping that through her God would give him a son. In those days, a man was permitted to have more than one wife, so Abram followed Sarai's advice. Hagar bore a son, whose name was Ishmael.

Years after Ishmael was born, God appeared to Abram and reassured him that His covenant still stood. Abram would indeed have many descendants, just as the Lord had promised. God said that he would no longer be known as Abram, but would now be called *Abraham,* which means "father of many nations." Sarai, his wife, would now be known as *Sarah,* which means "princess." God promised to bless Sarah with a son, whom they would call Isaac. God declared that nations and kings would spring forth from Isaac.

God also warned Abraham that his descendants would live for a time in a land of strangers, who would make slaves of them and oppress them for many years. But in the end, they would come back to the land of Canaan.

Then one day, when Abraham was sitting at the door of his tent, he saw three strangers walking toward him. He knew at once that these were not ordinary men, and he went out to meet them. He suspected there was more to these travelers than met the eye.

Bowing low, he greeted them, saying, "My lord, if I have found favor in your sight, do not pass by your servant." Abraham offered his guests food and drink to strengthen them on their journey.

The strangers accepted the invitation, and Abraham hurried to have food prepared for them. Sarah baked cakes of meal, and Abraham selected the best calf of his flock, giving it to a servant to prepare for cooking. When the meal was ready, it was set before the guests. Abraham stayed with them while they ate.

One of the guests told Abraham that Sarah would soon have a son. After hearing this, he knew God Himself was speaking to him. When the guests were ready to leave, Abraham walked a part of the way with them. They went toward the city of Sodom.

Sodom and Gomorrah

As they walked together, God told Abraham that the cities of Sodom and Gomorrah would be destroyed because of the sins of those who lived there. Abraham thought of Lot and the other good men of the city. So he tried to bargain with God.

He asked God: "Will you indeed destroy the righteous with the wicked? Suppose there are fifty righteous within the city; will you then destroy the place and not spare it for the fifty righteous who are in it?" Abraham could not believe that the Lord he loved so much would deliver such a horrible fate to the decent people within the city, even if they were far outnumbered by the wicked people.

God replied, "If I find at Sodom fifty righteous in the city, I will spare the whole place for their sake."

Still walking with the Lord, Abraham pressed further. He asked, if there were only forty-five or even forty righteous in the city, whether God would spare the whole place. And God answered yes.

Abraham pressed even further. He asked, if there were only thirty righteous in the city, whether God would spare the whole place. And God answered yes again.

Pressing yet even further, Abraham asked, if there were only twenty righteous, whether God would spare the whole place. And God answered yes. Finally, Abraham asked, if there were only ten righteous in the city, whether God would spare them all. And God answered yes. Then the Lord departed, and Abraham returned home.

But the sad fact was that there were not even ten righteous people in the cities of Sodom and Gomorrah.

That same evening, two of the strangers came to Sodom and saw Lot sitting at the gates of the city. Lot, not knowing they were angels, invited them to come with him and be his guests. They declined his invitation, but he persisted, so they accepted. He made a feast for them and baked unleavened bread, and they all ate together.

While they were eating, a crowd of wicked men, inhabitants of the city, came to the house to injure Lot's guests. But the angels struck them blind, leaving them helpless and unable to cause harm.

Then the angels told Lot that they had been sent by the Lord to destroy the city of Sodom. They advised him to leave at once, taking with him his loved ones. Lot had two daughters whom he had promised in marriage to two young men of the city. He went immediately to these young men and pleaded with them to leave the city, taking his daughters with them. But the young men wouldn't listen to him. When he insisted, they still refused to go.

In the morning, the angels told Lot to get up and take his wife and two daughters out of the city. Otherwise, they would die with the others when the city was destroyed. But Lot still hesitated.

So the angels took his hand, and the hands of his wife and daughters, and led them out of the city. The angels told them, "Flee for your life; do not look back or stop anywhere in the valley; flee to the hills, lest you be consumed." Lot begged to be able to take refuge in a nearby town instead, and the angels agreed.

THE STORY OF THE BIBLE—THE OLD TESTAMENT

Then the Lord rained down flaming sulfur on Sodom and the neighboring city of Gomorrah. The cities and all the country around them were destroyed, along with all the people who lived there, and the trees and other vegetation as well.

As they ran away, Lot's wife was curious to see what was happening. In spite of the angels' warning not to turn around or stop, she looked back. Her disobedience led to instant disaster: She was turned into a pillar of salt!

The next morning, Abraham went out to the high place where he had stood when he had talked with God about Sodom. From there, he could see the land in the distance where Sodom and Gomorrah had once stood. The smoke from their fiery destruction billowed up like the smoke from a terrifying furnace. But God had saved Lot and his family for Abraham's sake.

Abraham's Sons: Isaac and Ishmael

When Abraham was one hundred years old, and Sarah was ninety, God's promise to them was at last fulfilled: They had a son, whom they named Isaac. Through Isaac, Abraham's faith in God was rewarded. Under the watchful eyes of his parents, the boy grew strong and holy. He was the joy of his father's heart.

As a little boy, Isaac played around his father's tent with Ishmael, the other son of Abraham. You may recall that Ishmael's mother was Hagar, the Egyptian servant of Sarah. Sarah had become jealous of Hagar, and she didn't like to see the two boys playing together.

Sarah finally demanded that Abraham send Ishmael and his mother away. Hearing this, Abraham became very sad, and he didn't know what to do. Ishmael was just as much his son as Isaac was, and he loved him dearly.

God told Abraham to listen to Sarah and not to worry about Ishmael and Hagar. God promised that he would take care of Ishmael. Because the boy was Abraham's son, he too would grow up to become the father of a great nation.

The next morning, Abraham got out of bed early. He gave bread and a bottle of water to Hagar and sent her and her boy away. Heartbroken, she went out and wandered in the wilderness for days.

Much later, the water in the bottle was all gone. She saw Ishmael becoming weaker and weaker. Hagar was sure that he was dying of thirst and weariness.

Tenderly, she laid him down behind a bush and walked away, for she couldn't bear to see her son suffer and die. She rested under a tree and wept for her dying son. From where she sat, she could hear the boy crying as well, and she only wept more bitterly.

But the voice of an angel of God called to Hagar all the way from heaven, telling her not to be afraid. God had heard the voice of the child and would save him. He told her to pick up the boy again and hold him close. God had plans to make him a great nation.

Then God opened Hagar's eyes so that she could see a well of water nearby. Going to it, she filled the bottle and gave it to the boy to drink. He was refreshed once more.

God was with Ishmael as he grew up and lived in the wilderness of Paran. He became highly skilled with the bow and arrow and was known all over the country as a great archer. His mother chose a wife for him, a woman from the land of Egypt. Ishmael had twelve sons and a daughter who went on to marry Esau, the son of Isaac.

God Tests Abraham
One night, Abraham heard the voice of the Lord calling him. He answered, "Here am I."

The Lord replied, "Take your son . . . whom you love, and go to the land of Moriah, and offer him there as a burnt offering upon one of the mountains of which I shall tell you."

Abraham rose and saddled his donkey. He awakened two of his servants and Isaac. He cut wood for the sacrifice and, loading it on the donkey, set out on their journey.

They had traveled three days when Abraham saw in the distance the mountain God had chosen. He commanded his servants to stay behind with the donkey, while he and Isaac went up the mountain to make the sacrifice. He took the wood for the sacrifice and gave it to Isaac to carry, while Abraham himself carried fire and a knife. Together they started out for the mountain.

After a while, Isaac noticed that they had everything they needed for a sacrifice—except for a lamb. Where, he wondered, was the animal to be sacrificed? Abraham assured his son that God would provide the lamb when the time came.

When they reached the place that God had shown him, Abraham built an altar and laid the wood on it. He then tied up Isaac and placed him on the pile of wood. As he was raising his knife to sacrifice his son, an angel of the Lord called to him from heaven: "Abraham! Abraham!"

He answered, "Here am I."

The angel said, "Do not lay your hand on the lad or do anything to him; for now I know that you fear God, seeing you have not withheld your son."

Abraham paused and looked up. There in a nearby thorn bush, he saw a ram caught by the horns. So he took Isaac off the altar and offered the ram as a sacrifice to God instead of his son.

Then the angel repeated God's promise to Abraham: "Because you have done this, and have not withheld your son . . . I will indeed bless you, and I will multiply your descendants as the stars of heaven and as the sand which is on the seashore. And your descendants shall possess the gate of their enemies, and by your descendants shall all the nations of the earth bless themselves, because you have obeyed my voice."

Soon after this, Sarah died in Hebron. Abraham grieved and wept for his deceased wife, who had died at the age of one hundred and twenty-seven years. Abraham bought a field in a neighboring town, where a cave stood facing Mamre. He buried her within the cave and mourned her for quite some time.

For many readers of the Bible, Abraham is one of the more likable characters in the Old Testament. There's a reason why we often call him "our father in faith." We see from the moment Abraham enters this story that he held an unwavering faith in the Lord. Though he was quite old, he believed God's promise that he would have a son.

We also see Abraham's sense of loyalty when he looked out for the well being of Lot, his nephew. His generosity was shown by his desire to show hospitality to total strangers. And his compassion was displayed when he pled for the lives of those in Sodom, even though many of the people there were wicked.

Even so, God asked Abraham to do something that most of us could never imagine doing. Why would the Lord ask this faithful man to sacrifice his son Isaac? He did it to test Abraham's faith and obedience.

The Lord had promised Abraham that his descendants would be as countless as the stars in the sky. Abraham knew that this multitude of sons and daughters were to come through his son Isaac. Since Isaac had no children at this time, Abraham had to trust: either that Isaac would not die on this day, or that if he did, the Lord would find a way to raise him from the dead. So Abraham attempted to carry out the Lord's commandment with complete obedience.

We can only imagine the turmoil in his mind and heart as Abraham took his son, whom he loved and cherished, to the mountaintop and bound his hands. Consider as well how Abraham did all this without lying to his son. When Isaac asked where the lamb for the sacrifice was, Abraham assured him that God would provide a lamb when the time came. Abraham's faith was rewarded when God told him not to carry through with the sacrifice of Isaac, then provided a ram for the altar instead.

This moving story doesn't just show us the unwavering faith and obedience of Abraham. It also serves as a *foreshadowing*—an image of things to come. When we see this father about to sacrifice his son, it points to that day, many years later, when God our Father offered His only Son as a sacrifice for us all, the Holy Lamb of God.

Isaac Marries Rebecca

Before Abraham died, he sent Eliezer, his servant, to Haran to find a bride for Isaac. Some of Abraham's relatives still lived in Haran, and he wanted his son to marry someone from among his own people. So the servant took camels and many gifts with him.

When Eliezer arrived at Haran, he waited at a well outside the city where the women came to draw water. He called on God for help, hoping that God would find a way to fulfill Abraham's request to find his son a wife.

Eliezer prayed, "Let the maiden to whom I shall say, 'Please let down your jar that I may drink,' and who shall say, 'Drink, and I will water your camels'—let her be the one whom You have appointed for Your servant Isaac. By this I shall know that you have shown mercy to my master."

Eliezer was asking for a sign from God, to help him see which woman he was to find for Isaac.

Soon, Rebecca, a lovely woman, came to the well. She filled her pitcher and was going back home when Eliezer ran to meet her and asked her for a drink of water.

She put down her jar and replied, "Drink, my lord." After giving him a drink, she went on: "I will draw for your camels also, until they have done drinking." That task required Rebecca to fill her jar many times and empty it into the animals' trough.

Seeing this sign from the Lord, Eliezer was filled with joy. He gave her golden earrings and bracelets. He asked her who she was and whether he could stay as a guest at her father's house.

As it turned out, her family was in fact among those who were Abraham's own people. Rebecca told him that she was the daughter of Bethuel, and that they had plenty of room for both Eliezer and his camels. Then she ran home to tell the family about him, so they could prepare to offer him hospitality.

After Rebecca's family had welcomed Eliezer, they sat down to eat. But Eliezer would not eat until he had explained why he was there. When he told them how he was in search of a bride for his master's son, and that his meeting with Rebecca was an answer to his prayer, they allowed her to go with him back to Canaan. Eliezer gave presents to Rebecca, to her brothers, and to her mother.

The next morning they set out for Canaan. Isaac was the first person to greet them when they arrived home, and with the blessing of Abraham, he married Rebecca.

Then, thirty-eight years after Sarah's death, when Abraham was one hundred and seventy-five years old, he took his last breath and died as a very old man. He left all his wealth to his son Isaac, who was the child through whom God's promise was to be fulfilled. Isaac and Ishmael, his sons, buried him in the cave beside his wife.

CHAPTER 4

Jacob, the Son of Isaac

Jacob Steals His Brother's Birthright

Many years passed before Isaac and Rebecca had any children. Then, twins were born to them, two sons, whom they named Esau and Jacob. Esau, who was born first, grew up to be a large man, rough and hairy. He was a hunter and a farmer.

Jacob, the younger son, was more like his mother, gentle and quiet. He became a herdsman. Isaac favored Esau, and Rebecca favored Jacob. She had been told by God that the younger son would be greater than the older, and that the older son would serve the younger.

This was strange for Rebecca to hear, for in those days, the oldest son always received what was called the *birthright*. He was given a larger portion of his father's wealth than the other children, and he became the head and priest of the family. He also obtained a special blessing from his father before he died.

Esau, though he was the older brother, didn't care much about the birthright. But Jacob did. One day, Esau came home hungry from hunting. Jacob was cooking a stew of lentils.

The delicious smell of the stew made Esau feel even more hungry. He asked for some. But Jacob bargained with him, saying he would give his older brother some food only if Esau would give up his birthright.

Esau was more concerned about his hunger than his birthright. He thought so little of his birthright that he swore an oath to sell it to Jacob for some stew. Then he ate the bread and stew that Jacob gave him, and went on his way.

The years went by, and Isaac grew old. His eyes were dim, and he couldn't see. One day, he called for Esau.

"I am old," he said; "I do not know the day of my death. Now then, take your weapons, your quiver and your bow, and go out to the field, and hunt game for me, and prepare for me savory food, such as I love, and bring it to me that I may eat; that I may bless you before I die."

Rebecca overheard this conversation. After Esau had gone, she called for Jacob. She told him to bring in food for his father, and she would prepare it so that Jacob could deliver the meal to him. That way, the blind old man would mistake Jacob for his brother, and Jacob would be the one to receive his father's blessing.

But Jacob objected: "My brother Esau is a hairy man and I am smooth man. Perhaps my father will feel me, and I shall seem to be mocking him, and bring a curse upon myself and not a blessing."

Jacob worried that his father, though he was blind, would still be able to tell the difference between his two sons. Then Jacob would be caught trying to trick his father. But Rebecca assured him that everything would work out.

So Jacob brought the food to his mother, and she cooked a meal that she knew would please Isaac. She brought out Esau's best clothes and put them on Jacob, the son that she loved best. She covered his smooth neck and hands with the little skins of the animals Jacob had brought. Then she gave him the meat she had cooked and some bread she had baked, and told him to take them in to his father.

When Jacob entered the room, Isaac asked who was there.

Jacob lied, saying: "I am Esau your firstborn. I have done as you told me; now sit up and eat of my game, that you may bless me."

Isaac questioned how the young man had found the food so quickly, but Jacob brushed off the question by claiming that God had helped him find the game quickly.

Then Isaac said, "Come near, that I may feel you, my son, to know whether you are really my son Esau or not." Jacob approached his father. Isaac felt his arms, covered with a furry goatskin. He said, "The voice is Jacob's voice, but the hands are the hands of Esau."

Isaac was confused, hearing a voice that sounded like his younger son, but feeling what seemed to be the hairy hands of his older son. He questioned Jacob again, asking who he was, and Jacob lied again, saying he was Esau. After Isaac had eaten the meat and drunk the wine that Jacob offered him, he asked Jacob to come closer, so that he could receive a kiss from his son.

Jacob came near and kissed his father. A moment later, Isaac blessed him, saying:

"May God give you of the dew of heaven, and of the fatness of the earth, and plenty of grain and wine. Let peoples serve you, and nations bow down to you. Be lord over your brothers, and may your mother's sons bow down to you. Cursed be everyone who curses you, and blessed be everyone who blesses you!"

Jacob left quickly after receiving the blessing. He had been gone only a short while when Esau returned, bringing with him the meat from the animal he had hunted and killed. He asked his father to stand and take the food he had brought in, so that his father could bless him.

Isaac was terribly confused, asking, "Who are you?"

Esau answered plainly, "I am your son, your firstborn, Esau."

Isaac shook with anger, wondering aloud who had brought him food earlier. It became clear to both of them that Jacob had tricked Isaac into getting the blessing that Esau was entitled to have. Esau cried out bitterly, asking whether he could also receive a blessing.

Isaac answered, "I have made him your lord, and all

his brothers I have given to him for servants. . . . What then can I do for you, my son?"

Esau broke down and wept as though his heart would break. He asked again for his father to bless him. Isaac's heart was touched with pity for Esau, and he said to him:

"Behold, away from the fatness of the earth shall your dwelling be, and away from the dew of heaven on high. By your sword you shall live, and you shall serve your brother; but when you break loose you shall break his yoke from your neck."

From that moment on, Esau hated Jacob for having taken away his father's blessing. He swore that after his father's death, he would kill his brother.

When Rebecca heard that Esau had threatened to kill Jacob, she sent for her son and told him to flee to Haran, where her brother, Laban, lived. She instructed him to stay there until the fury of his brother had died down. When Esau gave up seeking Jacob to kill him, Rebecca would send for him.

Rebecca told her husband, Isaac, that Jacob was going away to find a wife among her own people. She insisted that she was afraid her son would marry some Hittite woman in the region where they lived. Rebecca didn't like the Hittite women. So Isaac sent for Jacob and blessed him, urging him to find a wife in the lands where Rebecca was sending him.

Many stories of treachery are told in the Bible, and this is one of the most famous. It's also one of the sadder stories, because the treachery here involves members of the same family, rather than enemies of war. Poor Isaac, with his failing health and eyesight, was tricked by his own wife and son.

The fatherly blessing isn't a common practice today, so we might wonder why it was so important in biblical times. In fact, it was a very important rite of passage in the family in those days, a ritual treated with the utmost honor and respect. It couldn't be given out at will to just anyone who wanted it.

This means that what Jacob and his mother did was a great injustice, both to Esau and to Isaac. And just as it is with all acts of treachery, the truth was eventually brought to light.

It's not easy to understand why God allowed Rebecca and Jacob to take the birthright away from Esau by deceit. But we can say that God knew it would happen: He had told Rebecca before Jacob was born that the younger brother would rule over the older. In any case, both Jacob and Rebecca eventually suffered because of the lie they had told.

In a sense, Rebecca lost both her sons that day. No doubt Esau deeply resented what she had done. Their relationship would never again have been the same. In fact, their dealings with each other were troubled at best: Esau married two Hittite women who made life bitter for both his parents.

Meanwhile, Jacob—the only son in whom Rebecca took pleasure—was forced to flee because of their lie. She was never again to set eyes on him. Jacob spent long years in hard labor far from his father's home, and when he finally returned, his mother had passed away.

In the end, however, despite all the bad that came from what he and his mother did, Jacob still had an important destiny waiting for him.

Jacob's Dream
Jacob traveled alone on the way to Haran. One night, he had a strange and mysterious experience. He was asleep on the ground, with a stone for a pillow, when he saw

in a dream a ladder reaching from earth to heaven. Angels were moving up and down the ladder, and God was standing above it.

The Lord said to Jacob: "I am the Lord, the God of Abraham your father and the God of Isaac; the land on which you lie I will give to you and to your descendants; and your descendants shall be like the dust of the earth, and you shall spread abroad to the west and to the east and to the north and to the south; and by you and your descendants shall all the families of the earth bless themselves. Behold, I am with you and will keep you wherever you go, and will bring you back to this land; for I will not leave you until I have done that of which I have spoken to you."

When Jacob awoke, he was filled with awe to realize that the Lord had met him in the place where he had slept. In memory of his dream, Jacob poured oil on the stone on which he had slept and called the place *Bethel,* meaning "House of God."

Jacob Meets Rachel and Returns to Canaan

When Jacob arrived at Haran, he met some shepherds near a well outside the city. He asked them whether they knew Laban, his mother's brother. While he was talking to them, Rachel, the daughter of Laban, came to the well to give water to her father's sheep. The shepherds told Jacob who she was.

While Jacob helped with her sheep, he told her they were cousins. Rachel hurried to her father and told him the news of Jacob's coming. So Laban went at once to meet Jacob and to welcome him to his house.

For a month Jacob was Laban's guest. After that, he began to work for Laban, taking care of his sheep. Laban promised that if Jacob worked for him seven years, he could have Rachel for his wife.

Jacob agreed to these terms. But at the end of seven years, Laban didn't keep his word. He tricked Jacob into taking his elder daughter, Leah, in marriage instead. But Jacob was not nearly as attracted to Leah as he was to Rachel.

Jacob complained to Laban about his deceit, for he was deeply in love with Rachel. He begged to be allowed to marry her. Laban finally promised to give him Rachel's hand in marriage within a week, but only if he agreed to work for seven more years. Jacob agreed, married Rachel, and worked another seven years for Laban.

After more than fourteen years of absence, Jacob was eager to return home, but Laban wanted him to stay. Jacob remained six years longer, in return for a certain share of the flocks. He had become rich in Laban's service and owned many sheep and goats. This caused Laban and his sons to envy him.

Then God spoke to Jacob and told him to return to the home of his fathers. Jacob now had eleven sons and one daughter. The sons were Reuben, Simeon, Levi, Judah, Dan, Naphtali, Gad, Asher, Issachar, Zebulon, and Joseph. His daughter's name was Dinah.

One day while Laban was away from home shearing his sheep, Jacob took his family, his flocks, and his goods, and set out for Canaan. Laban didn't learn of Jacob's departure until three days later. At once he set out in pursuit. He caught up to Jacob in the mountains and rebuked him, saying he would gladly have gone with him had he not left in secret.

Before Laban and Jacob separated this time, they set up a heap of stones. They prepared a meal and ate it on the heap, then made a solemn agreement never to pass this spot to injure each other or their possessions. Jacob called the heap *Galeed,* or "The Witness Heap."

Esau and Jacob Reconcile

When Jacob drew near to his native land, he sent messengers to his brother, Esau. With them, he sent camels, cattle, and sheep as gifts to gain his favor. Jacob hoped to make peace with him after leaving on such bad terms many years before. He even told the messengers to tell Esau that Jacob would become his servant.

When the messengers brought back word that Esau was coming with four hundred men, Jacob was terrified. He divided his company into two groups, thinking that if one company were wiped out, the other might escape. Then Jacob asked the Lord to protect him.

During the night, he gathered up his family and sent them across a stream with all that he owned. Jacob was then alone beside the stream. Suddenly, a stranger confronted him. The stranger wrestled with Jacob all through the night, until the first light of morning.

But Jacob could not be overcome. So the stranger said to Jacob, "Let me go, for the day is breaking."

Jacob answered the stranger, "I will not let you go, unless you bless me."

Then the stranger, who was really an angel, asked, "What is your name?"

"Jacob," he replied.

The angel said in return, "Your name shall no more be called Jacob, but Israel, for you have striven with God and with men, and have prevailed."

Then the angel disappeared, and Jacob called the place *Peniel,* meaning "the face of God." He said, "For I have seen God face to face, and yet my life is preserved."

The next day Jacob saw Esau coming in the distance. He ran forward and bowed down before him, pleading forgiveness for the lie he had told so many years ago. But Esau was no longer angry. He lifted up his brother and kissed him. Jacob offered him gifts of sheep and other animals. At first Esau was unwilling to accept them, but finally, to please Jacob, he took them.

After Esau had departed, Jacob crossed the Jordan and passed on to Shechem, which is in the land of Canaan. Here he bought land for the price of a hundred lambs. At God's command he stayed for a time at Bethel, where he had seen the vision of the ladder. He built an altar there and offered a sacrifice to God.

Next Jacob went to Bethlehem, where his youngest son, Benjamin, was born. Here also his wife Rachel died. Jacob mourned for her and built a monument over her grave.

From Bethlehem, Jacob returned to his father, Isaac, who lived near Hebron. He remained with Isaac until the old man died. Esau and Jacob buried their father in the cave at Mamre, where Sarah, Abraham, and Rebecca were buried.

At the death of Isaac, Jacob inherited the share of the firstborn son. In time, he was to become the *patriarch*, or father, of a great nation. But Jacob's family had to undergo many adventures and endure many trials for that nation to be born. The next stage in their remarkable journey was deeply shaped by the life of one of Jacob's sons, a gifted young man called Joseph.

CHAPTER 5

Joseph, the Son of Jacob

Joseph's Humble Beginnings

Jacob's sons were herdsmen, spending their lives tending their sheep and goats. Their work often took them far away from home, where their father couldn't keep an eye on what they were doing. One day, Joseph saw his brothers doing wrong. He went home and reported it to his father, and from that time on they resented him.

But there were other reasons why Joseph's brothers didn't like him. They knew that their father loved Joseph very dearly, and when he gave the boy a fine coat of many colors, they became very jealous. Joseph also reported his dreams to his brothers, dreams that foretold his future greatness and the power he would one day have over them. Not surprisingly, these dreams angered the brothers.

Joseph told about his first strange dream, in which he and his brothers stood in a field bundling up grain. Joseph claimed that his bundle was the largest and stood upright, while his brothers' bundles of grain all bowed before it. Joseph interpreted this to mean he would one day rule over his brothers. They resented his dream and his words about it.

Then Joseph reported another dream to his brothers. He claimed that he saw the sun, moon, and eleven stars bowing before him. This implied that not only his brothers, but even his father and mother would bow down to him. Once again, his brothers wanted to hear nothing of it. Joseph seemed to be saying that he would one day become their king.

Some time later the brothers were forced to travel great distances from home to find grass for their flocks. While they were at Shechem, a place fifty miles from their home, Jacob sent Joseph out in search of them, to find out if all was well. When Joseph reached Shechem, he learned that his brothers had driven their flocks ten miles farther north, so he kept going.

When the brothers saw Joseph coming, they hatched an evil plan to kill him. But Reuben, the oldest brother, wanted to save Joseph from death. He persuaded the others to throw him into a pit, hoping to have an opportunity later to help Joseph escape.

It happened that some merchants, who were on their way to Egypt, were passing through the fields. The brothers stopped the merchants and offered to sell Joseph to them as a slave. The merchants offered twenty pieces of silver in exchange for Joseph. This sum satisfied the brothers, and Joseph was led away to Egypt.

While this was going on, Reuben was far away in another part of the field. When he learned what had happened, he was terribly upset. He knew that his father would place all the blame for the evil deed on him, since he was the oldest of the brothers.

In order to save Reuben from their father's anger, the brothers decided to deceive Jacob. They dipped Joseph's brightly colored coat, the one their father had given him, into the blood of a goat. They sent it to their father and told him they had found it by the roadside.

Jacob believed that Joseph had been killed by a wild beast. He was filled with grief, and could not be comforted by his other sons.

Joseph in Egypt
When the merchants brought Joseph to Egypt, they sold him to the chief captain of Pharaoh's guard, a man named

Potiphar. Before long, Potiphar saw that Joseph was the best of his servants, so he placed him in charge of his house. Under Joseph's management, Potiphar's fortune grew, and he became wealthier day by day.

But Potiphar's wife was a wicked woman. She found Joseph attractive, for he was a handsome young man. But Joseph wouldn't do wrong in order to please her.

So she went to her husband and falsely accused Joseph of sin. Potiphar was furious. He didn't try to find out the truth, but believed what his wife said. He cast Joseph into prison.

The keeper of the prison was moved by God to look with favor on Joseph. He placed him in charge of the other prisoners.

After some time, Pharaoh's butler and baker aroused his anger. They were cast into the prison where Joseph was in charge. Joseph saw that they were troubled one day and asked why they were sad.

"We have had dreams," they answered, "and there is no one to interpret them."

Joseph knew that God could grant him the proper interpretation. So he replied, "Tell them to me, I beg you."

The chief butler was the first to tell about his dream:

"In my dream there was a vine before me, and on the vine there were three branches: as soon as it budded, its blossoms shot forth, and the clusters ripened into grapes. Pharaoh's cup was in my hand; and I took the grapes and pressed them into Pharaoh's cup, and placed the cup in Pharaoh's hand."

Joseph interpreted the dream for the butler:

"The three branches are three days; within three days Pharaoh will lift up your head and restore you to your office; and you shall place Pharaoh's cup in his hand as formerly, when you were his butler."

Joseph then asked the butler to remember him when he was back at the Pharaoh's side, explaining that he had wrongly been thrown into the prison.

Next, the baker told about his dream:

"I also had a dream: there were three cake baskets on my head, and in the uppermost basket there were all sorts of baked food for Pharaoh, but the birds were eating it out of the basket on my head."

Joseph interpreted the dream for the baker:

"The three baskets are three days; within three days Pharaoh will lift up your head—from you—and hang you on a tree; and the birds will eat the flesh from you."

Pharaoh's birthday was three days after Joseph had explained these dreams, and a great feast was prepared for the celebration. At the banquet, he remembered the chief butler and restored him to his office. But the baker he hung on a scaffold. In this way, both of Joseph's interpretations had come true.

When the butler was leaving the prison to return to the side of Pharaoh, Joseph had reminded him, "Remember me, when it is well with you, and do me the kindness, I pray you, to make mention of me to Pharaoh, and so get me out of this house. For I was indeed stolen out of the land of the Hebrews; and here also I have done nothing that they should put me into the dungeon."

But after the butler was released from prison, he forgot all about Joseph.

At this point, Joseph must have been wondering what God had in store for him. The young man believed, because of the special dreams he'd had as a boy, that he was destined for greatness. But here he was, confined in an Egyptian prison, betrayed by his brothers and falsely accused of wrongdoing by his employer's wife.

When Joseph successfully interpreted the dreams of

the butler, he must have hoped that his time had come to leave this dreadful place at last. Surely, this man would return to Pharaoh and tell him about the young man who could read dreams. But that was not to be—at least, not yet. The butler quickly forgot about Joseph, and he remained in prison.

Joseph must have come close to despair in that prison cell. But eventually, it was again a dream—this time, dreamed by the Pharaoh himself—that would turn Joseph's life upside down.

Pharaoh's Dreams

About two years later, Pharaoh had a dream in which he stood by the Nile, the great river of Egypt. Seven cows came out of the river, beautiful and fat. But seven other cows followed them, looking thin and sickly. Then the lean cows ate the fat cows. Yet still after eating so much, the cows remained thin and gaunt.

Pharaoh then had a second dream. He saw seven ears of grain come up from one stalk, plump and good. After this, seven other ears sprang up on the same stalk, thin and blasted by the east wind. The seven thin ears ate all the plump and good ears.

Pharaoh could find no one in his kingdom who could explain these strange dreams to him. It was then that the butler remembered Joseph in prison. He told Pharaoh how Joseph had explained his own dream and that of the baker, and how his interpretations had proven true.

Pharaoh at once commanded that Joseph be brought before him to explain the dreams that no one else could. Before Joseph began to interpret Pharaoh's dreams, however, he told the ruler that the power to interpret dreams comes from God alone. Then Joseph said the two dreams foretold the same thing.

"God has revealed to Pharaoh what he is about to do," Joseph insisted. "The seven good cows are seven years, and the seven good ears are seven years; the dream is one. The seven lean and gaunt cows that came up after them are seven years, and the seven empty ears blighted by the east wind are also seven years of famine."

Joseph went on with his interpretation. "There will come seven years of great plenty throughout all the land of Egypt, but after them there will arise seven years of famine, and all the plenty will be forgotten in the land of Egypt; the famine will consume the land, and the plenty will be unknown in the land by reason of that famine which will follow, for it will be very grievous. And the doubling of Pharaoh's dream means that the thing is fixed by God, and God will shortly bring it to pass."

Joseph then advised Pharaoh to appoint a wise man to prepare for the famine. His duty would be to store away one fifth of all the grain raised during the seven fruitful years, so that when the famine came, there would be enough food saved up for everyone.

Joseph Becomes Governor
Pharaoh was very grateful to Joseph and much pleased with him. He wondered how he could find a man wiser than Joseph, so he appointed him governor. Joseph was second only to Pharaoh in the kingdom.

Pharaoh put his ring on Joseph's finger and clothed him in a rich robe. He put a chain of gold around his neck and called for the second finest chariot in the kingdom, ordering that Joseph was to be driven through the streets of the city. A man was sent ahead to proclaim to all the people that Joseph was made governor over the whole land of Egypt, and that they should bow their knee before him.

The country that Joseph would rule over occupied the northeastern corner of Africa. It included the delta and the valley of the Nile River. The valley is about five hundred miles long and from ten to thirty miles wide. The Red Sea and the Arabian peninsula are on the east of this fertile strip, and the Mediterranean Sea is on the north.

The fertility of Egypt depended on the overflow of the Nile each year. This annual flood had to reach the height of twenty-five feet to insure good crops for the season. If the flood were lower than eighteen feet, the crops failed, and famine followed.

This is why, in Pharaoh's first dream, the cows who represented the harvest came up out of the Nile. Whether the harvest was plentiful or blighted depended on how high the great river flooded.

Joseph went on to marry Asenath, the daughter of Potiphera, a priest of On. This marriage gave Joseph a high social standing, because the priests belonged to one of the highest classes among the Egyptians. Two sons were born to him. The older, he called Manasseh; the younger, Ephraim.

The seven years of plenty came, and Joseph traveled through every part of the country, overseeing the building of great granaries. These large structures would store one fifth of all the grain produced. In all the great cities, food from the surrounding fields was gathered up and preserved for the people.

But as Joseph had prophesied, seven years of famine followed those of plenty. Nothing grew throughout the land. Soon, the people began to ask Pharaoh for food, but he sent them all to Joseph and told them to do as he instructed.

The famine increased daily and spread beyond Egypt. Joseph opened up the granaries and began to sell grain to the Egyptians. But they had no money, so they gave their land instead. Through these deals, Pharaoh became the owner of almost all the land in Egypt during these years of famine.

Joseph Meets His Brothers Again

The famine spread to the land of Canaan, and Jacob and his family were among those who suffered. Hearing that there was grain in Egypt, Jacob sent ten of his sons to buy enough to care for their needs. Benjamin, his youngest son, he kept at home, to keep him safe.

When the sons of Jacob came to Egypt, they were sent to Joseph the governor. Joseph had changed a great deal in appearance and manner since the day his brothers had sold him to the merchants of Egypt. So they didn't recognize him—but Joseph recognized his brothers.

In order to test them, Joseph spoke harshly to them and accused them of being spies. They tried to convince him of their innocence, telling of their father and their youngest brother, whom they had left at home. They also told him about Joseph, another brother, who was dead. They had no idea it was Joseph they were talking to at that very moment!

They explained that they had come to Egypt to buy grain because of the famine in Canaan. But Joseph pretended not to believe them. He cast them all into prison and kept them there for three days. Then he released all but one: Simeon. This brother, he said, would have to remain in prison until the others brought to him, as a proof of their good intentions, the brother they had left at home.

The brothers spoke among themselves in their own language, right in front of Joseph. He had been speaking to them in the language of the Egyptians, through an interpreter, so they didn't know he could understand them. They admitted among themselves that they deserved to be treated in this way for their sin against their brother so many years ago. It seemed to be God's justice.

Secretly, Joseph wept for joy to see his brothers repent of their sin, though they didn't know he was aware of the whole story. Even so, Joseph still insisted that Simeon remain in prison, and he bound the young man as they watched. Then Joseph commanded his servants to fill the sacks of the others with the grain they had purchased.

Without his brothers' knowledge, however, Joseph told the servants to place in their sacks the money his brothers had paid for the grain. In addition to the supplies of grain, he also gave them provisions for their journey. But they didn't discover what had been done until they stopped along the way home to spend the night.

When the brothers arrived in Canaan, they told their father, Jacob, all that had happened. When they asked him to let Benjamin go to Egypt with them in order to set Simeon free, Jacob refused. He had lost one son, and the second was in prison. He would not risk losing a third.

However, it wasn't long before the family of Jacob again needed grain, for the famine was still going on. Reluctantly, he asked his sons to go to Egypt and buy it. Judah told his father that it would be useless to go without Benjamin. He was certain that the ruler of Egypt would not receive them unless they had Benjamin with them. When Judah promised his father that no harm would come to Benjamin, Jacob consented to let him go.

At their father's instruction, they took back with them the money they had found in their sacks. They were ready as well to give Joseph gifts and double the amount they needed to buy more grain. They wanted to make certain Benjamin and Simeon would return.

When Joseph saw his brothers returning with Benjamin, he ordered his servants to prepare a feast. Then Simeon was released from prison and presented to them. Joseph spoke with his brothers, asking if their father was in good health. At one point, as he laid eyes on his youngest brother, Benjamin, he was so overcome with joy that he went into his room and wept. Yet still, after all this, Joseph's brothers didn't recognize him.

After the feast, Joseph told his servants to fill his brothers' sacks with grain. Again he commanded them to place in their sacks the money they had paid. But he also had another plan.

"Put my cup," he told his servant, "the silver cup, in the mouth of the sack of the youngest, with his money for the grain."

The next morning, the brothers departed early for Canaan with their heavy sacks, not knowing all that Joseph and his servant had done. After his brothers had gone some distance, Joseph sent his chief servant after them. When the servant caught up to them, he asked why they had returned evil for good, and accused them of stealing his master's silver cup.

They knew nothing about the silver cup. They were so certain they didn't have the cup that they made a proposal: If any one of them had it, he should be put to death. They added that they were ready to become Joseph's slaves if the servant found the cup in any of their sacks.

They took down their sacks from the animals that carried them and opened them without hesitation or fear. But they all recoiled in shock and terror when the silver cup fell out of Benjamin's sack!

The servant ordered them to return to Joseph. When they entered the house, Joseph asked them why they had tried to steal his silver cup. But they didn't know how to

answer. All fell to their knees, bowing low before Joseph, and offered themselves as his slaves. This act was in fact a fulfillment of the dreams Joseph once had as a boy.

Joseph said that he wanted only the man who had stolen his cup as his slave—that is, Benjamin. But Judah pleaded with the governor, telling him the story of the brother they had lost so many years ago, one named Joseph. He said that the loss of Benjamin would be too great a sorrow for his father to bear, and would certainly cause his death. Judah offered himself as a slave to Joseph in Benjamin's place.

At this point Joseph could no longer hide his identity. He asked all the Egyptians to leave the room. When he was alone with his brothers, he spoke to them in their own language, amidst tears of joy.

"Come near to me, I beg you. I am your brother, Joseph, whom you sold into Egypt. And now do not be distressed, or angry with yourselves, because you sold me here; for God sent me before you to preserve life."

Joseph went on to explain how it was God's will that he had been sent to Egypt to save his father and brothers from the famine. Then he sent his brothers back to their father to tell him of his success in Egypt, and to invite his father to come with all his family to live in the land of Goshen, a district within Egypt.

Pharaoh was pleased with Joseph's invitation to his father and his brothers. So he sent wagons to Hebron to move their possessions to Egypt. He gave presents to all the brothers, but he was especially generous to Benjamin. To Jacob he sent clothing made of the finest material, along with three hundred pieces of silver.

Joseph Meets His Father

When Joseph learned that his father was on the way, he rode in his chariot to meet him.

The reunion of father and son after so many years of separation was a great joy for both of them. They embraced each other and wept.

"Now let me die," Jacob said to his long-lost son, "since I have seen your face and know that you are still alive."

Joseph took his father and brothers to Pharaoh, who gave to Jacob the land of Goshen.

Jacob went on to live in Egypt seventeen years. One day, word was brought to Joseph that his father was sick. He set out at once to see him, taking with him his two sons, Manasseh and Ephraim. When Jacob heard that Joseph was coming, his strength returned, and he sat up in his bed to greet him.

Seeing Manasseh and Ephraim, he asked, "Who are these?"

"They are my sons," Joseph answered, "whom God has given me here."

"Bring them to me, I pray you, that I may bless them."

When they came close to him, Jacob kissed and embraced them, and gave them a blessing.

Then Jacob called his sons around his bed and foretold all that would happen to them and their descendants. To each he told what awaited in their future. Some of his prophecies told of greatness, and others of shame.

When he had finished speaking to his sons, Jacob lay back on the bed and died. Joseph ordered his father's body to be embalmed in the manner of the Egyptians. Then he asked Pharaoh's permission to take the body back to Canaan for burial, for Jacob had asked his son to bury him in the place of his ancestors. Pharaoh gave his permission and sent them off.

The body of Jacob was carried in a great procession to the land of Canaan. All the princes of Pharaoh's court and the leading men of the land of Egypt went with them. They buried him in the double cave with Abraham and Sarah, and Isaac and Rebecca. Rachel, the mother of Joseph and Benjamin, was buried at Bethlehem.

Joseph lived fifty-four years after his father's death. He prophesied that Jacob's people would leave the land of Egypt, and he left orders for them to carry his bones with them when they did.

Joseph's story is important for many reasons, especially because it shows us that God has a purpose for everything. How many times must Joseph have wondered what God had planned for him? Think of him as he sat in that jail cell. Could he possibly have imagined that one day soon he would be the governor of Egypt, saving his brothers from a famine—the very same brothers who had sold him into slavery?

But that's exactly what happened. Joseph's path was guided by God's hand, who put him in the place he needed to be for each day of his life.

If Joseph hadn't been sold into slavery all those years ago, he would never have become the servant of Potiphar. If Potiphar hadn't thrown him into prison for a crime he didn't commit, he would never have interpreted the dream of the butler. If he had never interpreted the butler's dream, he would never have been called on to interpret the Pharaoh's dream, and he would never have become governor of Egypt. Without becoming governor, he couldn't have prepared the people for the famine, or saved his brothers and father from starvation.

God finds marvelous ways to weave together our lives with such beauty, if only we'll trust in Him! But as we'll see in the stories ahead, not everyone trusted in God the way Joseph did.

PART THREE

How God Protected His Chosen People
and Led Them Into the Promised Land

CHAPTER 6

God Calls Moses to
Lead His People

The Origins of Moses

After Jacob wrestled with the angel, God gave him the new name Israel. So the descendants of Jacob came to be called the *Israelites*. But they were also known in the Bible as *Hebrews*, especially in the story of Moses, and eventually they were known as *Jews*.

For some time after Joseph's death, the Hebrews continued to enjoy freedom and prosperity in Egypt. While the descendants of Lot and Esau were leading a nomadic life in the areas surrounding Canaan, Jacob's descendants were living in peace and growing in power and wealth in Egypt. The descendants of each of Jacob's sons became an entire tribe. Together they came to be called the twelve tribes of Israel.

But finally a new Pharaoh ascended the throne—one who was not friends with Joseph's people. Then everything changed, and the life of the Hebrews became very hard. They were enslaved and forced to make countless bricks for Pharaoh's great building projects. No longer a happy people, the Hebrews became sad and weary in the service of the Egyptians.

What brought about this change in their condition? The new Pharaohs were jealous of the power and wealth of the Hebrew people. They feared that these settlers from Canaan might still have close ties to other peoples outside of Egypt who were rivals for Egyptian power and wealth. In addition, the Pharaohs needed slave laborers to build their temples, canals, and cities.

Why did God allow these great sufferings to afflict His chosen people? To answer that question, we must note that the hearts of the people had changed even before they became slaves to Pharaoh. In their time of freedom and happiness, many of them had fallen into imitating the evil ways of the Egyptians. The Hebrews often worshipped the false gods of Egypt instead of the true God of Abraham, Isaac, and Jacob.

The hard lot to which the Pharaohs subjected the Hebrews made them refocus their thoughts on God to ask for His help. When they did, their years in Egypt came to an end. According to the promise made by God to Abraham, the time for their return to Canaan was at hand. That wonderful departure from slavery in Egypt is called the *Exodus*.

In spite of all they had to undergo, the Hebrews in Egypt constantly increased in number. Pharaoh feared that they might rise up in revolt against him. To keep down the number of those who could bear arms in battle, Pharaoh ordered that every Hebrew boy should be killed as soon as he was born.

This order of Pharaoh was not always obeyed, because Hebrew families found ways to protect their babies. Many little boys were saved, and among them was one called Moses.

For three months the mother of Moses concealed him at home. But as he grew, she feared that he might be discovered. So she made him a wicker basket and covered it with tar so it would be waterproof. She placed the baby in the basket and set it down among the reeds that grew close to the banks of the Nile River. Then she pushed it away, downriver, praying to God to take care of her little boy.

Miriam, the older sister of Moses, stood at a distance, watching to see what would happen to her little brother. Now, just at that moment the daughter of the cruel Pharaoh, with her maidservants, approached the river to bathe in it. Pharaoh's daughter saw the basket, and she ordered one of her maids to bring it to her. When she uncovered it, she found the poor, crying baby.

"This is one of the Hebrews' children," she said.

Miriam, at a distance, trembled for the safety of her brother. But when she saw that the princess looked lovingly at the babe, she ran up to her.

"Shall I go and call you a nurse from the Hebrew women to nurse the child for you?" she asked.

The princess agreed, so Miriam went and got her mother. The princess, not knowing the woman, placed Moses in his own mother's care, and promised to pay for her services to the child.

When Moses was older, the princess took him to live with her in the palace. There he was educated as a prince. He ate the best kind of food and wore the finest clothing. Under private teachers, he learned to read and write the picture language of the Egyptians. He studied arithmetic, learned how to survey the land, and came to understand the religious beliefs and different social classes of the Egyptians.

We should consider for a moment the remarkable plan God had for Moses. Though the boy was doomed to die by the Pharaoh's command, the Lord rescued him and had him raised as a prince in that same Pharaoh's palace. It was God's strategy to train Moses there for leadership: not as the ruler of Egypt, but as the champion of God's chosen people, who would lead them out of slavery back home to the land of their ancestors.

For his destiny to be fulfilled, Moses had to grow up in Pharaoh's court. But one day, his world of privilege and comfort came to a sudden end.

Moses Flees From Egypt

Though Moses lived like a prince, he never forgot his mother and other relatives. He loved his own people, the Hebrews, and it pained him to see how harshly they were treated.

One day when Moses had grown to manhood, he was walking in the neighborhood of the palace. A number of Hebrews were hard at work under an Egyptian boss. The boss became angry at one of the Hebrews and began to mistreat him cruelly. When Moses saw this mistreatment, he was filled with rage and killed the Egyptian.

The news of the killing soon reached Pharaoh. He ordered that Moses should be put to death. But Moses escaped and fled to a place called Midian, in the region of Mount Sinai.

On his way, he sat down by a well to rest. While he was there recovering his strength, seven daughters of a priest named Jethro came to water their flocks, but some shepherds drove them away. Moses defended the girls, and when they told their father what had happened, he invited Moses to his house.

Jethro begged Moses to remain with him and help him with his flocks. Moses agreed and lived with him forty years. During that time he married one of Jethro's daughters, Zipporah, who bore him several sons. During these forty years God prepared Moses for the great position of leader of His chosen people. His life in the open air, tending the grazing flocks, must have made him healthy and strong.

The Burning Bush

One day while Moses was tending his flocks near Mount Horeb, he saw a bush in flames. Yet strangely enough, the bush did not burn up. Moses approached it so he could look closer at this mystery.

Suddenly, a voice spoke to him from the flames: "Moses, Moses!"

He answered, "Here am I."

"Do not come near," the voice continued; "put off your shoes from your feet, for the place on which you are standing is holy ground. . . . I am the God of your father, the God of Abraham, the God of Isaac, and the God of Jacob."

Moses hid his face, for he was afraid. But the voice of God went on.

"I have seen the affliction of my people who are in Egypt, and have heard their cry because of their taskmasters; I know their sufferings, and I have come down to deliver them out of the hand of the Egyptians, and to

bring them up out of that land to a good and broad land, a land flowing with milk and honey. . . . Come, I will send you to Pharaoh that you may bring forth my people, the sons of Israel, out of Egypt."

Moses answered, "Who am I that I should go to Pharaoh, and bring the sons of Israel out of Egypt?"

"I will be with you," God answered; "and this shall be the sign for you, that I have sent you: when you have brought forth the people out of Egypt, you shall serve God upon this mountain."

Then Moses asked, "If I come to the sons of Israel and

say to them, 'The God of your fathers has sent me to you,' and they ask me, 'What is his name?' what shall I say to them?"

The Lord answered, "I AM WHO I AM. Say this to the sons of Israel, 'I AM has sent me to you. . . . The Lord, the God of your fathers, the God of Abraham, the God of Isaac, and the God of Jacob, has sent me to you.' This is my name for ever, and thus I am to be remembered throughout all generations.

"Go and gather the elders of Israel and say to them, 'I have observed you and what has been done to you in Egypt; and I promise that I will bring you up out of the affliction of Egypt." Then the Lord promised again to bring them to a land flowing with milk and honey.

But Moses replied, "They will not believe me or listen to my voice, for they will say, 'The Lord did not appear to you.'"

Then God gave Moses three signs he could use to prove that he was to be their leader. First, he turned Moses' staff into a serpent, and then back again into a staff. Then, he told Moses to put his hand to his chest, and when he did, his hand was covered with leprosy, as white as snow. When Moses put his hand back to his chest, his hand was healed again.

Finally, God told Moses that if the people still wouldn't believe, then he was to take some water from the Nile River and pour it on the dry land. As they watched, it would turn into blood.

But Moses still hesitated. He objected that he couldn't speak well, and he was afraid to approach Pharaoh. So God appointed Aaron the Levite, Moses' brother, to speak for him. But Moses was to tell him what to say.

Moses returned to Jethro and, taking his wife and two sons, set out for Egypt. On the mountain of the burning bush, he met Aaron, whom God had led there. Moses explained to Aaron all that God had told him. Then they both returned to Egypt.

Moses and Aaron Arrive in Egypt
As soon as Moses and Aaron arrived in Egypt, they began to carry out God's instructions. They gathered the Hebrews around them and told them how God had appointed them to be their leaders. They told the people of the wonderful things that had happened on Mount Horeb, and showed them the signs God had given them to prove their mission.

The Hebrews believed Moses and Aaron and accepted them as their leaders. They were ready to follow them out of the land of Egypt into the Promised Land, the land of Canaan that God had promised to give them.

Then Moses and Aaron went to Pharaoh. They asked him to give the Israelites a period of three days' rest from their slave labors. During that time, they would journey into the wilderness to offer sacrifice to their God.

But Pharaoh wouldn't listen to such a request. Why should he allow the slaves to be idle for three days? Pharaoh feared the Hebrews, and he wasn't anxious to preserve their health and strength. So he sent Moses and Aaron away and told them never to annoy him again.

Angered by this visit, Pharaoh commanded his overseers—those in charge of the Hebrews—to place new burdens on the Hebrews. Straw was normally mixed into the clay used to make bricks, to hold it together. Now, the overseers forced the Hebrew slaves to gather the straw as well as make the bricks.

Much time was lost in gathering the straw. So the Hebrews weren't able to make as many bricks as they had before, when someone else was supplying the straw. Yet the Egyptian overseers demanded as many bricks as before, and they cruelly whipped those who couldn't produce that many.

Some of the chief laborers of the Hebrews went to Pharaoh and begged for relief from their new duties and burdens. But Pharaoh's heart was cold. He mocked and laughed at them, saying they shouldn't have asked for three days off to journey into the wilderness and make a sacrifice to their God.

When these laborers met Moses and Aaron, they blamed them for making the burdens of the people heavier. They complained that the two of them shouldn't have approached Pharaoh and made such a request for their days off.

Moses and Aaron were discouraged. They prayed to God again, and He told them to be patient. He promised Moses and Aaron that the time of their freedom from bondage was near. But the people were sad and weary, and they didn't listen to what Moses and Aaron told them.

Again God sent the two brothers to Pharaoh to demand that he let the Hebrews leave the land of Egypt. He told Moses to show Pharaoh the amazing signs He had given to him.

When Moses and Aaron appeared before Pharaoh again, Aaron took the staff and threw it on the floor. It was turned into a serpent. Pharaoh called for his magicians, and they performed the same act, turning all their staffs into serpents. But the serpent from Aaron's staff swallowed up the other serpents, and it became a staff again in Aaron's hand.

Even then, Pharaoh would not listen to the words of Moses and Aaron. He refused to let the Hebrews go.

The Ten Plagues
God spoke to Moses again. "Pharaoh's heart is hardened," the Lord said; "he refuses to let the people go. Go to

Pharaoh in the morning, as he is going out to the water; wait for him by the river's brink, and take in your hand the rod which was turned into a serpent. And you shall say to him, 'The Lord, the God of the Hebrews, sent me to you, saying, "Let my people go, that they may serve me in the wilderness; and behold, you have not yet obeyed."'"

Moses and Aaron did as they were told. As Pharaoh was watching, Aaron lifted his staff and struck the river. Immediately, the water was turned to blood. The river was polluted, the fish died, and the Egyptians couldn't drink the water.

There was blood in all the land of Egypt. This was the first of the plagues sent by God.

But Pharaoh's magicians also turned the water into blood. So Pharaoh refused to believe the sign, and his heart was hardened. He wouldn't do as the Lord commanded by letting the people of Israel leave Egypt.

When this plague had lasted seven days, God commanded Moses and Aaron to go to Pharaoh again and request that the Hebrews be allowed to leave. If Pharaoh still wouldn't allow it, God warned that the entire land would be covered with frogs, including the houses, beds, and kitchens of all the Egyptians and their servants. But Pharaoh wouldn't listen.

When they went out from Pharaoh's presence, Aaron raised his staff over the waters, and at once the land was overrun with frogs. But the magicians also caused frogs to come forth on the land.

This time Pharaoh sent for Moses and said to him, "Entreat the Lord to take away the frogs from me and from my people; and I will let the people go to sacrifice to the Lord."

Moses believed Pharaoh and asked God to remove the plague. In answer to his prayer, all the frogs died. They were gathered together in heaps, and the land was filled with their rotting bodies.

Pharaoh Refuses to Keep His Promise

When Pharaoh saw that the plague had ended, he refused to let the people of Israel leave Egypt. Then Aaron struck the dust of the earth with his staff, and God sent a plague of gnats that caused great discomfort. The magicians attempted to do the same, but they could not. So they went to Pharaoh and told him, "This is the finger of God." But Pharaoh was stubborn and still wouldn't budge.

At the command of God, Moses met Pharaoh early in the morning at the river bank and demanded that he let the people depart. Pharaoh refused yet again. So a fourth plague, one of flies, was sent on all the land of Egypt, except for Goshen, where the Hebrews lived.

Pharaoh then called Moses and Aaron and said, "Go, sacrifice to your God within the land."

Moses refused, knowing that if they were to sacrifice the animals *within* the land of Egypt, the Egyptians would surely stone them in anger for killing cattle, which they considered sacred. He knew they had to depart from this land and go into the wilderness.

Pharaoh finally agreed to let them leave, so Moses prayed that the plague of flies would be taken away. And it was so. But after this occurred, Pharaoh went back on his word, deceiving Moses yet again. He still would not let the people go.

So Moses came to Pharaoh again. He told him that if he didn't let the Hebrews leave Egypt, all the camels, oxen, horses, and sheep in the whole land, except those in Goshen where the Hebrews lived, would be afflicted with disease and death. Pharaoh was filled with bitterness and refused again. Then all the animals of the Egyptians died, but those of the Hebrews were unharmed. Despite this clear sign from God, Pharaoh still wouldn't let the people of Israel leave.

Egypt Suffers Worse Plagues

For this reason, God brought even worse troubles on Pharaoh and his people. This time, all the people, as well as the animals, were stricken with boils—nasty bumps and scars that covered their skin. The plague spread over all the land, and the suffering was very great. But Pharaoh refused to obey the word of the Lord.

Moses went to Pharaoh and threatened another plague if he didn't yield to God's will. This time it would be damaging hail. Once more Pharaoh refused, and a great hailstorm with thunder and lightning swept over the land. It beat down the crops and destroyed the houses. Only the land of Goshen was spared.

When Pharaoh saw all the destruction, he promised to let the Israelites go into the wilderness if the storm would stop. Moses went outside the city and stretched out his hands. The storm stopped. But Pharaoh was unfaithful to his promise, just as he had been before.

Moses and Aaron next threatened Pharaoh with a plague of locusts that would destroy whatever crops were left. The servants of Pharaoh came and begged him to let the Hebrews leave, so that no more harm would come to Egypt. Pharaoh said he would let the men leave, but he wouldn't let the women and children go.

He knew that if the women and children stayed behind, the men would be forced to return after completing their sacrifice. Then Pharaoh would have all his slaves back. But if the men's families came with them to the wilderness, they might not return.

Moses couldn't agree to Pharaoh's terms. So the eighth

plague followed, and great swarms of locusts filled every field of crops, eating up every blade of grass.

Pharaoh sent for Moses and Aaron once more. He promised to grant them their wish if they would remove the plague. They prayed, and a strong wind came and swept all the locusts into the Red Sea. But after the plague was gone, Pharaoh's heart was hardened again, and he refused to let them leave.

Yet a new plague came, with darkness covering the land, even in the middle of the day. Pharaoh's servants and all the people were terrified. Pharaoh called for Moses and Aaron and told them to go. Not only the men, but also the women and children could go. But he commanded them to leave their flocks in Egypt, for he was trying once more to make sure they would return.

Moses told the Pharaoh that they needed the animals as victims for the sacrifice. But Pharaoh would not yield. He told Moses that if he ever came into Pharaoh's presence again, he would have him killed.

CHAPTER 7

The Escape from Egypt

The Final Plague

God told Moses that He would bring one last plague on the Egyptians, a plague so terrible that Pharaoh would be forced to let the people of Israel go. To prepare for their departure, the Lord commanded the Hebrews to ask their Egyptian neighbors for gifts of gold and silver. These gifts were actually payment for the hard labor the people of Israel had performed for so many years.

The Egyptians had come to respect the Hebrews because of the astonishing things Moses had done. They were afraid to refuse their request, so they gave them all that they asked. In this way, before their departure from Egypt, the people of Israel were no longer poor slaves. They possessed gold, silver, and valuable clothing.

Even though the Hebrews received such wonderful gifts from the Egyptians, the Pharaoh still wouldn't allow them to leave. So the greatest plague, the tenth and final one, came on them.

The Lord said to Moses, "Yet one plague more I will bring upon Pharaoh and upon Egypt; afterwards he will let you go from here; when he lets you go, he will drive you away completely."

This last plague was to be the worse. God instructed Moses to tell Pharaoh that all the firstborn children of the Egyptians, even Pharaoh's son himself, would die. In addition, the firstborn of all the cattle would die as well. But the Hebrew children and cattle would not be touched.

Such a drastic threat angered Pharaoh terribly. He still refused to let the people of Israel leave.

The First Passover

Seeing that Pharaoh still wasn't listening to the messages, Moses went back to the Israelites. He told them what God had said to do during this tenth and final plague.

Moses said to them, "Select lambs for yourselves according to your families, and kill the Passover lamb. Take a bunch of hyssop and dip it in the blood which is in the basin, and touch the lintel and the two doorposts with the blood which is in the basin; and none of you shall go out of the door of his house until the morning.

"For the Lord will pass through to slay the Egyptians; and when he sees the blood on the lintel and on the two doorposts, the Lord will pass over the door, and will not allow the destroyer to enter your houses to slay you."

About midnight, the destroying angel of the Lord entered every Egyptian home, from that of Pharaoh to that of the lowliest man. The firstborn of every Egyptian family lay dead. But seeing the blood of the lamb sprinkled on the doorposts of the Hebrews, the angel passed over their homes, and not a single Hebrew child was harmed.

This great sorrow finally softened the heart of Pharaoh. He summoned Moses and Aaron and told them to lead the people of Israel out of the land of Egypt without delay. The Hebrews had lived in Egypt four hundred and thirty years.

Ever since then, the people descended from Israel, now called the Jews, remember what God did for them so they could escape from Egypt. Each year they celebrate a great feast to commemorate the event, called the Passover, because the destroying angel passed over their homes that night.

Perhaps we would all do well to remember what happened so long ago in Egypt. Do you find yourself asking how Pharaoh could be so stubborn? Do you wonder why he kept breaking his word to Moses? Do you see how he tried to negotiate with God, offering at first to do part of what God commanded, but not all of it?

The truth is that, if we're honest, we probably can see at least a little bit of Pharaoh in ourselves. Even when it's clear what God wants us to do, we may be stubborn, not wanting to obey because it will cost us. Or we may promise the Lord that we'll do what He wants, but later break our promise. Then, when our disobedience leads to problems, we may try to negotiate with God about how much of His will we're willing to obey.

When we're tempted to respond to the Lord that way, we should remember Pharaoh's story. As we'll see, he still hadn't learned his lesson when he let the people of Israel leave. One last time he changed his mind, and he sent his army chasing after them. But through his pursuit of the Hebrews, Pharaoh provoked one of the greatest and most memorable acts of God ever recorded in the Old Testament.

The Departure

Six hundred thousand Hebrew men, plus their families, set out from Egypt that night with Moses and Aaron. They took with them all their possessions—their clothing, ornaments, vessels of gold and silver, weapons, and tents—as well as flocks of sheep and herds of cattle.

Before Joseph died, he had prophesied that the people of Israel would leave Egypt. He had made them promise to take his remains with them. Moses and the people remembered the promise their ancestors had made to Joseph, so when they left Egypt, they carried the body of Joseph with them.

To show them the way, the Lord appeared to them by day as a pillar of cloud, and by night as a pillar of fire. This was how He led them out of Egypt, choosing a route that would take them across the Red Sea.

Pharaoh soon regretted letting the Hebrews leave Egypt. He prepared his chariot and his entire army. With six hundred chosen chariots and all the captains of the army, he pursued the people of Israel.

He found them encamped by the shore of the Red Sea. Looking in the distance, the Hebrews saw the Egyptians coming after them. They were terrified, and they cried out to the Lord to help them. They told Moses that it would have been better to be slaves in Egypt than to be killed in the wilderness.

Moses relieved their fears when he told them: "Fear not, stand firm, and see the salvation of the Lord, which He will work for you today; for the Egyptians whom you see today, you shall never see again. The Lord will fight for you, and you have only to be still."

The Parting of the Red Sea

The cloud of God's presence had led the Hebrews to this point. Now it moved behind them to shield them

from the pursuing Egyptians. Moses prayed to God for more help.

God replied, "Why do you cry to me? Tell the people of Israel to go forward."

This was a strange thing for God to suggest, for the Red Sea, a long and deep arm of the ocean, stood directly before them. But God spoke to Moses further.

"Lift up your rod, and stretch out your hand over the sea and divide it, that the sons of Israel may go on dry ground through the sea."

Moses did as he was commanded. The waters of the sea were divided, and a strong wind dried a path. The Hebrews were amazed. They crossed this path to the opposite shore between two walls of ocean water.

While they were crossing, the pillar of cloud was lifted. The Egyptian armies, with all their chariots and horses, hurried after the Hebrews through the path. But by the power of God, their chariots were bogged down, and their journey through the two walls of water was delayed. The Egyptians cried out, "Let us flee from before Israel; for the Lord fights for them against the Egyptians."

But it was too late. As soon as the last Hebrew had crossed over to the opposite shore, God said to Moses, "Stretch out your hand over the sea, that the water may come back upon the Egyptians, upon their chariots, and upon their horsemen."

Moses did as God commanded. The waters closed in, and all the chariots and the Egyptian army were buried in the depths of the sea. The Hebrews were saved! In gratitude to God for their deliverance, Moses and the people of Israel sang a song of thanksgiving.

The Wilderness, the Quail, and the Manna

Now they could continue their journey in peace. On their way to the land flowing with milk and honey, the people of Israel had to travel through a desert. They had little food and even less water, and the country was strange and foreign to them.

The Israelites encamped at a place where they found a spring, but the water of the spring was bitter. So Moses called the place *Marah*, which means "bitterness." At the command of God, Moses cast a tree into the water, and the bitterness was taken away.

After a journey of six weeks, the Israelites reached the wilderness called Sin. Here they were sorely in need of food. They murmured against Moses and told him that they had been better off in Egypt than in the wilderness, for there they had food to eat, while in the desert they were starving. They seemed to think that as long as their bellies were full, it didn't matter whether they were slaves.

God heard the people complaining about their hunger. He said to Moses:

"Behold, I will rain bread from heaven for you; and the people shall go out and gather a day's portion every day, that I may test them, whether they will walk in my law or not. On the sixth day, when they prepare what they bring in, it will be twice as much as they gather daily."

The Lord also promised that the people would have meat to eat in the evening, to go along with the bread they would gather each morning. So Moses relayed what had been told him and promised the people that food would come.

That evening, God sent quail into the camp for them to catch and eat. In the morning, a heavy dew covered the earth. It looked like frost on the ground. When the Israelites saw it, they asked one another what it was, for they weren't familiar with it.

"It is the bread which the Lord has given you to eat," Moses told them. He went on to explain how they should gather each day a portion for that day, but on the sixth day they should gather two days' portions. That way, they wouldn't be working to gather food on the seventh day, the day of rest called the Sabbath.

Everyone gathered as much as he needed in the morning. The rest melted when the sun grew hot. The Israelites called this food *manna*.

It was white like the seed of a little flower, and it tasted like flour and honey. The people of Israel lived off this manna until they reached the borders of the land of Canaan. Every morning they gathered as much as they needed for the day. On Friday they gathered two portions, for on the following day, the Sabbath day, the manna wouldn't fall.

From the Wilderness of Sin the Israelites went to Rephidim and camped at the foot of Mount Horeb, where Moses had seen the burning bush. God had told Moses that after the people escaped from Egypt, he would return to this mountain. Now the Lord's promise had been fulfilled.

Even though God continued to keep His word, the people murmured once more against Moses. They were thirsty and had no water. So God commanded Moses to strike a rock. The rock was dry, but when Moses struck it, water gushed forth, and the thirsty people were satisfied.

Moses Reunites with His Family
At Rephidim, the Amalekites, a band of warlike nomads and descendants of Esau, attacked the Israelites and tried to rob them of their possessions. They didn't like the Israelites coming into their territory and using the land's resources. So Moses appointed a man named Joshua to choose men who could form an army to fight against these attackers.

When the battle was about to begin, Moses took the staff of God in his hand. He went up on the mountain with Aaron and Hur—another of the leading men—to pray for victory. Below them in the valley, the battle would be fought.

Moses held the staff up over his head while he prayed. Once he did this, a strange thing happened. As long as he held up the staff, the Israelites were successful. But the moment he lowered it, the Israelites gave way to their enemy. It seemed that the outcome of the battle was being determined by the staff in Moses' hand!

The battle was very long. When Moses grew weary, Aaron and Hur stood on either side of him and held up his arms. With their help, he was able to keep his arms extended until sunset. The Amalekites were defeated and driven off. So Moses built an altar to God in thanksgiving.

But this would not be the last battle between the Israelites and the Amalekites. A long series of wars would follow, as a deep hatred grew between them.

At Rephidim, Jethro, the father-in-law of Moses, came to meet him. He brought with him the wife of Moses and their two sons, who had been sent there from Egypt. Moses welcomed them with joy in his heart and led them to his tent. There, Moses told Jethro all that had happened since the Israelites had left Egypt. Jethro was overwhelmed by the favors the people were given by the Lord, so he offered a sacrifice to God in thanksgiving.

By this time, the people of Israel had begun bringing their disputes and quarrels to Moses, so that he could resolve them. But there were too many quarrels for one man to handle. While the people were camped at Rephidim, Moses accepted Jethro's wise advice to appoint other judges to take care of this responsibility.

Meanwhile, God knew that the people would need more than judges to help them live together in harmony. They were not yet a nation; they were simply a mass of freed slaves in search of a home. They needed wise laws to follow that would show them how to live together as a nation according to God's will. And that was the next great gift the Lord had in store for them.

CHAPTER 8

The Revelation of God's Law

Moses Receives the Commandments

When the Israelites left Mount Horeb, they journeyed to the valley at the foot of Mount Sinai. Here, they found springs of water and grass for their flocks. In this valley, they stayed for two years.

God did wonderful things for them in this place. He gave them the great Law according to which they and all peoples were to live. But before He gave them this law, He prepared them for it.

First, the Lord asked them whether or not they would be obedient to the Law. He promised them that if they were obedient, He would make them His chosen people. Next, God instructed them to consecrate themselves for two days—that is, to wash themselves and their clothes as a way of preparing to focus on Him in worship and prayer. Then, the Lord told them, on the third day He would come down on Mount Sinai in the sight of all the people.

When God was ready to give His law to the Israelites from Mount Sinai, He told Moses to draw a boundary line at the foot of the mountain. This line the people were forbidden to pass. All this was done so that the Israelites might know the importance of the Law they were about to receive.

On the third day, Moses led them out of their tents to the boundary line he had drawn. Lightning flashed across the sky, and loud thunder mixed with the shrill blast of a trumpet. Mount Sinai, which is nearly 8,000 feet high, was suddenly covered with a heavy cloud. Thick smoke rose from the mountain as it might from a furnace. The trumpet sound grew louder and louder, and an earthquake shook the mountain.

The people trembled with fear. As they waited, they heard God's voice proclaiming these Ten Commandments:

1. "I am the Lord your God, who brought you out of the land of Egypt. . . . You shall have no other gods before Me."
2. "You shall not take the name of the Lord your God in vain."
3. "Remember the Sabbath day, to keep it holy."
4. "Honor your father and your mother."
5. "You shall not kill."
6. "You shall not commit adultery."
7. "You shall not steal."
8. "You shall not bear false witness against your neighbor."
9. "You shall not covet your neighbor's wife."
10. "You shall not covet your neighbor's house . . . or anything that is your neighbor's."

The people were struck with fear and moved back from the voice. They said to Moses, "You speak to us, and we will hear; but let not God speak to us, lest we die." From then on, God spoke to the people only through Moses.

Then Moses went up into the cloud on the mountain-top where God was, and God spoke to him. God promised Moses that His angel would lead the Israelites into Canaan, the Promised Land. He ordered them to make no treaty with the inhabitants of Canaan, but to drive them out of the country.

Moses came down and told the people all the commands that the Lord had given him, and they promised to obey them. Then he wrote the words of God and built an altar. He chose young men from every tribe and had them sacrifice calves on the altar. Moses then poured half of the blood on the altar and sprinkled the rest on the people and the book he had written. This he did as a sign of the solemn covenant between God and His people.

A second time Moses was called by God up the mountain. This time, he took Joshua with him. Seven days after he climbed the mountain, God called him into the cloud, and there he remained for forty days and forty nights. It was then that God gave him, written on two tablets of stone, the commandments He had spoken to the people amid the thunder and lightning.

The Lord also gave Moses many instructions about how to worship Him. The body of laws that God gave the people through Moses, both about worship and about how to live a holy life, came to be known as *the Law of Moses.*

The Golden Calf

Moses stayed up on the mountain with God for so long that the Israelites feared he had abandoned them. They worried as well that God was no longer with them. So they decided to serve a different god.

The people collected their golden jewelry and brought it to Aaron. Then they forced him to make a golden calf like the one they had seen the Egyptians worshiping. When the golden calf was ready, the Israelites worshiped it and made a great feast in its honor.

God knew what was happening with the people. He said to Moses, "Go down; for your people, whom you brought up out of the land of Egypt, have corrupted themselves."

Moses came down from the mountain with the two tablets of the commandments. When he saw the people worshiping the golden calf and dancing around it, he was enraged. He threw the tablets of stone on the ground, shattering them into many pieces. He burnt the golden calf and beat it into powder.

As judge of the people, Moses sentenced to death those who had led the others into worshipping the idol they had created. He cried out, "Who is on the Lord's side? Come to me."

Immediately the sons of Levi stood by his side. At the command of Moses they drew their swords and slew the guilty and whoever came in their way. Twenty-three thousand men were killed. The rest of the people did penance, and God forgave them their sin.

God then commanded Moses to make two tablets like the first, replacing the ones he had shattered. These other tablets Moses took up to the mountain, and again God wrote on them the commandments. Moses remained on the mountain for forty days and forty nights. When he came down to the people, rays of light shone out from his face. The people were afraid to come near him, so he covered his face with a veil and told them all that he had learned while he was with God on the mountain.

Now that God had given His people the commandments to live by, He had to teach them how to worship Him. Some of the ways the Israelites worshiped will sound familiar to us. For example, worship was led by priests at an altar, and certain days were set aside to feast or to fast from food.

Other aspects of their worship may seem strange to us, such as sacrificing animals and not eating pork or shellfish. But God had His reasons for all the rules of worship He gave them. These rules kept the people from becoming too much like the nations that worshipped false gods. In addition, the ceremonies God instructed them to perform reminded them to be thankful and to be sorry for their sins.

In this way, the ancient worship of the Israelites pointed toward Jesus Christ, the Savior who was to come centuries later. When He came, He established a new covenant and a new people, the Church. The ways of worship that we're familiar with today developed in the Church in light of what Jesus had said and done to bring us all to God.

The Instructions from God

God gave Moses exact instructions about how the Israelites were to worship Him. Moses called on the people to make offerings of gold, silver, bronze, dyed skins, fine linen, acacia wood, and whatever else was necessary for the sacred vessels, the vestments of the priests, and the building of a *Tabernacle*—a great tent where the people gathered.

The response of the people was enthusiastic. All the needed materials were donated, and skilled workers in the various trades volunteered their services to construct everything as God had commanded.

The Tabernacle was the meeting place for worship, just as Christians meet today in churches. But it had to be carried from place to place by the Israelites during their time of wandering in the desert. So they had to make it in such a way that they could easily set it up, take it down, and carry it with them on their journey.

The Tabernacle was an oblong tent, forty-five feet long, fifteen feet wide, and fifteen feet high. The back and sides were made of acacia wood and covered with gold. They were held together by five poles of the same kind of wood, also covered with gold, which passed through five golden rings on each board. The boards rested in silver sockets.

Four coverings formed the roof. These coverings extended down over the sides. An inside covering of embroidered linen draped the walls. The outer coverings were made of goats' hair, along with rams' skins dyed red and violet.

At the entrance to the Tabernacle there were five pillars of acacia wood, overlaid with gold, and with golden capitals. These pillars were set in sockets of bronze. They supported an embroidered linen curtain, which acted as the door of the Tabernacle. Thirty feet beyond this were four similar pillars, from which hung another curtain to separate two areas: the *Holy of Holies,* which was a room containing a sacred box, called the *Ark of the Covenant;* and the *sanctuary,* or holy place.

In the sanctuary were kept *the altar of incense, the table of showbreads,* and *the seven-branched candlestick.* Here the priests performed their sacred functions.

The Tabernacle was erected at the west end of a long enclosure known as the *court of the Tabernacle,* one hundred and fifty feet long by seventy-five feet wide. It was fenced in by embroidered linen curtains supported on bronze pillars, with a special curtain at the entrance. The altar of holocausts, or burnt animal sacrifices, stood inside the entrance. Between it and the Tabernacle was the bronze basin, a large bowl of water where the priests purified themselves before they entered the Tabernacle.

The *Ark of the Covenant* was a large box made of acacia wood and lined inside and outside with gold. It was almost four feet long, just over two feet wide, and just over two feet high. Moses placed inside it the two stone tablets of the Law, along with a jar of manna. Later the staff of Aaron, the brother of Moses, was also placed in it.

The Ark's cover was of solid gold. On each end of it were two golden images of angels, whose wings covered the Ark. This cover was called the *mercy seat.* From then on, when God spoke to Moses, it was from a cloud that rested over the mercy seat. The Ark was the only thing placed in the Holy of Holies.

The *table of showbreads* was made of acacia wood and covered with gold. It was three feet long, one and a half feet wide, and just over two feet high. On each end of the table were placed six loaves of showbread, which were made of the finest flour, without yeast. The twelve loaves were replaced with new ones every Saturday as a constant offering of thanks to God.

The *altar of incense* was made of acacia wood covered with gold. There was a grating in the top surface. It was one and a half feet long, one and a half feet wide, and three feet high. It was placed before the veil of the Holy of Holies.

The *seven-branched candlestick* was hammered out of pure gold. It was made to light the sanctuary of the Tabernacle with seven lamps, which were to remain lighted continually. Its weight in gold was one hundred and thirty pounds.

The *altar of holocausts* was made of acacia wood and covered with bronze. It was seven and a half feet long, seven and a half feet wide, and four and a half feet high, and it had bronze horns at each corner. It was hollow, with a grating in the top surface. Beneath the grating there was a hearth for the fire and a pan to catch the ashes from the grating. This altar was placed just inside the entrance to the court.

The Priesthood

God told Moses that Aaron and his sons should be set aside for the worship in the Tabernacle. The firstborn son was to be high priest, and the other sons were to be priests. They alone were permitted to offer sacrifices to God on behalf of the people.

The high priest wore a long linen robe with sleeves that stretched all the way down to his feet. Over this robe, he wore another robe, this one sleeveless and reaching to his knees. This outer robe was comprised of four colors: violet, purple, crimson, and white. It was fringed at the bottom with golden bells and embroidered pomegranates.

The priest's outermost garment was called the *ephod*. It was something like a cloak of two parts. The ephod was fastened at the shoulders with two onyx stones, each one engraved with the names of six of the tribes of Israel. It was fastened at the waist by a belt.

Over the ephod was worn a *breastplate*, a square of cloth matching the ephod. On the breastplate were set twelve precious stones engraved with the names of the twelve tribes. This breastplate was fastened by golden chains to the shoulders and by a purple ribbon to the waist.

On his head the high priest wore a white linen *miter*, or crown-shaped cap. On it was fastened a gold plate engraved with the inscription "Holy to the Lord." The other priests wore only embroidered linen robes with cloth belts and the linen miter.

When the Tabernacle was finished, Moses brought Aaron and his sons to its entrance and washed them with water. He then dressed Aaron and his sons in priestly robes and consecrated the hands of Aaron's two sons. This ceremony lasted for seven days. In this way, Moses carried out God's commands, and Aaron and his sons were ordained priests for the people of Israel.

The whole tribe of Levi was assigned to help the priests, because of the devotion and loyalty they had shown to God when others had worshiped the golden calf. God provided a ceremony to initiate them into their new position.

They were sprinkled with water to purify them, and their hair was shaved from their heads. Then they were led into the court of the Tabernacle, where the people passed by them, placing their hands on the head of each one. This was a sign that the nation was giving to the Levites the duty of serving God in acts of public worship.

Two oxen were then brought before the Levites. On the heads of these oxen every Levite placed his hands. The oxen were then sacrificed. One was offered as a sacrifice for sin; the other as a burnt offering in adoration.

Kinds of Sacrifices

The Law of Moses prescribed two kinds of sacrifices. The first were the *unbloody* sacrifices, in which various kinds of plant foods were offered: the fruits of the earth, or flour, dried corn, and frankincense, together with oil and wine. The second was *bloody* sacrifices, in which animals were slain. These were young bulls, lambs, goats, or turtledoves, and all had to be without blemish.

The offerings, or *oblations,* of flour had to be mixed with salt, oil, and frankincense. The priest burnt a portion of these on the altar and retained the rest for his own use. At the same time an offering of wine was poured out at the foot of the altar.

The bloody sacrifices were of four kinds. *Holocausts* offered the entire animal victim to God by consuming it with fire. It was an act of adoration to acknowledge God's supreme dominion over the worshipper and everything he owned.

Peace offerings were made as acts of thanksgiving or petition. *Sin offerings* were made for lesser, or venial, sins. Finally, *trespass offerings* (also known as *expiatory* offerings) were given to make satisfaction for serious sins or restitution for injuries committed.

In these last three offerings, only the fat and entrails of the victim were burnt. The right shoulder and breast, which the priest waved before the Lord, were reserved for himself. The remainder of the animal was restored to the one who offered the sacrifice.

Every morning and evening the priests were required to offer a holocaust of a lamb for all the people. Incense also was offered every day on the golden altar of incense. On the Sabbath, the day of rest, two animal victims were offered at the sacrifices.

On the monthly feast celebrated at the new moon, many animal victims were slain, and the feast was announced by the blowing of silver trumpets. The new moon of the seventh month of each year was called the *Feast of Trumpets,* when a number of animal victims were sacrificed. Every seventh year was called the *sabbatical year,* when the land was to lie uncultivated, and sowing and reaping were forbidden.

Feast Days
God set aside certain days of the year when the Israelites were to honor Him with more prayers and sacrifices than usual. These days were known as *feast days.* God appointed these feast days because He wanted to remind His chosen people from time to time, in a special way, what kind of worship they owed to Him, and how many great deeds He had done for them in their history. In this way, their hearts would be moved to gratitude for all the favors God had shown them.

The *Day of Atonement* was observed on the tenth day of the seventh month of each year. It was the great day of public penance, when no work was done, nor was any food eaten. On this day, the high priest officiated. He laid aside his official vestments and clothed himself in a plain white linen garment, like that of the other priests, with a cloth belt and a head covering. This was the one

time of the year in which he was permitted to enter the Holy of Holies.

When the people were assembled in the morning, he sacrificed a calf. He entered the Holy of Holies, offered incense, and sprinkled the mercy seat seven times with the blood of the calf. This sprinkling of blood was to makes amends for his sins and the sins of the priests.

When he came back to the court of the Tabernacle, two goats were brought before him. One of these he chose by casting lots. He sacrificed it and sprinkled the blood in the same way he had sprinkled the blood of the calf. On the head of the second goat, the one not chosen, he laid his hands and confessed the sins of the people over it. Then he ordered this second lamb to be led out into the wilderness. From this practice, we get the English word *scapegoat*.

After this ceremony, the high priest washed and dressed in his usual robes. He then offered two rams to adore God, the Owner of all things. One of these he offered for himself, and the other for the people.

The first of these special days in the calendar of the Israelites was the *Feast of the Pasch,* or *Passover,* also called *Azymes* (unleavened bread). It was celebrated on the fourteenth day of the first month, called Nisan (March-April). As we have noted, this feast was appointed by God to recall to the Israelites the night they had sprinkled blood on their doorposts for protection from the destroying angel. That event had ultimately freed them from slavery and death and allowed them to leave Egypt.

In the evening of this day, the Israelites ate the *Paschal* lamb (the lamb of the *Pasch*) in their tents. They roasted the lamb with formal rites and ceremonies, and ate it with unleavened bread and bitter herbs. They ate while standing and dressed in their traveling clothes, each with a traveling staff in hand. The celebration lasted for eight days, but work was forbidden only on the first and last day of the ceremonies.

About seven weeks (fifty days) later, the *Feast of Pentecost* was celebrated. Two loaves of bread made from the new wheat of the harvest, and two spring lambs, were offered as sacrifices. This was a day of thanksgiving for the harvest and the increase of the flocks. It also honored God's giving of the Law on Mount Sinai. The people were forbidden to labor on this day as well.

On the fifteenth day of the seventh month began the *Feast of Tabernacles* (or *Feast of Booths*), which lasted for seven days. It was celebrated in thanksgiving for the fruit harvest, and in memory of the Israelites' dwelling in tents during their wanderings in the wilderness. During these days, more sacrifices were offered than during any other feast. On the first and last day of this feast, labor was forbidden.

All these ancient worship rituals of the Israelites were the roots of the religious traditions practiced by the Jewish people today. They also serve in many ways as the roots of our Christian worship, because Jesus Christ was the fulfillment of God's promise to His chosen people. Through the Tabernacle, sacrifices, priestly ministry, feasts, and fasts of the Jewish people—and also through the Scriptures that, in time, God inspired them to write and revere—the Lord prepared the way for Christ and for the rites of worship that would be practiced by His Church.

In the Law of Moses, God gave His people the foundation for a new life as a happy and prosperous people. But it wasn't long before some of the Israelites began to complain again and to rebel against God's plan for them.

CHAPTER 9

The Desert Wanderings
of the Israelites

Departing From Mount Sinai

For two years the cloud that guided the Israelites through the wilderness hung over the Tabernacle. Moses took a census of the people at the command of God; he was to count them and separate them according to their tribes.

The men who were twenty years of age and older were counted, except for those who belonged to the priestly tribe of Levi. There were 603,550 of them. In addition, there were many women, children, and youth. There were also people who weren't Israelites but had joined them on their journey. So all in all, their numbers were far greater than the census counted.

After the census was complete, the cloud of God's presence lifted into the heavens as a sign that once again, the time had come to travel on. It began to move slowly in the direction where the Lord wanted the Israelites to follow.

The priests blew the silver trumpets as a signal to the people to pack up their tents. Aaron and his sons took down the Tabernacle and packed it up for the march. They removed the veil that hung before the Ark of the Covenant and covered the Ark with it. The carrying poles were put into the rings on the sides of the Ark, and two violet coverings were placed over the veil.

The table of showbreads, the seven-branched candlestick, the altar of incense, and the altar of sacrifice were carefully and reverently covered, in preparation to be carried on the shoulders of the Levites. Six wagons were needed to carry the hangings, the pillars, and the planks of the Tabernacle.

When all was ready, the march began. Some of the Levites carried the Ark of the Covenant at the head of the procession, with the priests following. The tribes of Judah, Issachar, and Zebulon were next in line, while behind them were the wagons carrying the material of the Tabernacle. The tribes of Reuben, Simeon, and Gad followed; then came the rest of the Levites, carrying the sacred furniture of the Tabernacle. The remaining tribes marched in the following order: first Ephraim and Manasseh, who were the two tribes descended from Joseph's two sons; and then Benjamin, Dan, Asher, and Naphtali.

After a march of about three days, the Israelites were tired and began to murmur complaints against the Lord. They were bitter that they had been forced to undergo this journey. God heard their complaints and was angered at their lack of faith. He sent down fire that destroyed many of them and caused the rest to repent and beg forgiveness for their lack of faith in Him. Moses prayed fervently for them, and the fire was taken away.

But not long afterward, new complaints arose. These were sparked by strangers who had come with the Israelites from Egypt. The strangers were very persuasive, and the Israelites joined them in a rebellion against Moses.

The people yearned for the few comforts they had known back in Egypt, even though their lives had been bitter there as slaves. They had grown tired of the manna that the Lord fed them daily, and they complained that they had no fresh meat to eat. To appease them, the Lord sent a strong wind into their camps that brought with it a great number of quail they could kill and eat.

This provision restored the peace, but only with a price. A plague broke out among the people while they ate the quail, and a number of them died. Because of their ingratitude to God, they would never see the land that He had prepared for them.

Soon a new revolt occurred. Even Moses' sister, Miriam, and his brother, Aaron, the high priest, rebelled against Moses. They seemed to be jealous of Moses' good standing with the Lord.

"Has the Lord indeed spoken only through Moses?" they asked the people. "Has he not spoken through us also?"

God heard their grumbling and was not pleased. He punished Miriam for her sin by striking her with leprosy. Her skin appeared dead and as white as snow. Aaron was terrified, and Moses begged God to cure her. He did, but her punishment lasted seven days, and she was kept outside the camp for fear that others might get her sickness.

For a while after this rebellion, there was peace among the people. The Israelites marched on toward the Promised Land, and at last they reached the border of Canaan.

Spies and a Rebellion

Before they entered Canaan, God commanded Moses to choose twelve men, one from each tribe, and to send them as scouts, or spies, into the land. Moses selected the twelve, and among them were Joshua, from Ephraim, and Caleb, from Judah.

Moses said to them, "Go up into the hill country, and see what the land is, and whether the people who dwell in it are strong or weak, whether they are few or many, and whether the land that they dwell in are camps or strongholds, and whether the land is rich or poor, and whether there is wood in it or not. Be of good courage, and bring some of the fruit of the land."

The scouts traveled all over the land of Canaan for forty days. At Hebron they found a great cluster of grapes. It was so large that, when they cut it off the vine, it took two men to carry it. They also took pomegranates and figs from that place and brought them back to where Moses and their people waited.

All the people gathered together with Moses and Aaron to listen to their report. The scouts said, "We came to the land to which you sent us; it flows with milk and honey, and this is its fruit. Yet the people who dwell in the land are strong, and the cities are fortified and very large."

Hearing this, the people became frightened. They didn't want to enter a land that was occupied by so many great and powerful people, living in large and guarded cities. They began to speak out against Moses.

But Caleb, in order to quiet them, said, "Let us go up at once, and occupy it; for we are well able to overcome it."

The other scouts disagreed. They said again how strong the inhabitants of Canaan were. They claimed the Israelites would be no match for them.

When the discontented people heard this report, they refused to go any farther. They told Moses they didn't want him as their leader. So they decided to elect a captain to lead them back to Egypt.

This act was a great sin, because it was rebellion against God and His plan for them. Joshua and Caleb tried to calm the people by advising them to go forward and conquer the land, but they couldn't persuade them. The people even threatened to put Joshua and Caleb to death!

Moses and Aaron prayed that God would spare the people in spite of this great sin of disobedience. God heard their prayer, but the ten scouts, who by their report had caused fear in the people and sparked the rebellion, were struck dead by a plague. Joshua and Caleb had made a favorable report, so they were spared.

The rest of the Israelites were also punished for this and all their other rebellions. All who were over twenty years of age were condemned to linger in the desert until they died. Only Joshua and Caleb were allowed to enter the Promised Land, because of their faithfulness to God.

But the spirit of revolt and rebellion continued. Some of the Israelites attempted to invade Canaan against God's command, trying to enter on their own when they saw Moses would no longer lead them in. But God was not with them, and the Amalekites, who had fought with the Israelites before and lived near the border, killed many of them and drove back the rest.

After this defeat, the Israelites knew that they couldn't escape the punishment of God. They were doomed to wander in the desert until death. But some were still disobedient.

Three men named Korah, Dathan, and Abiram, with two hundred and fifty leaders of the people, spoke out against Moses and Aaron and challenged their authority. They tried to perform the duties of the priests, but the earth opened up and swallowed them and all their possessions.

Others sought to injure Moses and Aaron, but they fled to the Tabernacle for safety. God sent a plague to destroy all the rebels and save Moses and his brother.

Now that the leaders of the revolt had been removed, peace was restored. To show the people that this peaceful spirit pleased Him, God caused Aaron's wooden staff to bloom miraculously, as if it were a living bush bursting with buds. This was a sign that Aaron's priesthood placed him above all the other leaders except Moses. After this miracle, the staff of Aaron was placed in the Ark of the Covenant.

The Last Years of Moses
The Israelites wandered about Kadesh, an area not far from the southern border of the Promised Land. During these wanderings, Miriam, the sister of Moses, died and was buried at a place called Cades.

About this time the people complained because they lacked water. Moses and Aaron went into the Tabernacle and fell flat on the ground to pray for the people. God said to Moses, "Take the rod, and assemble the congregation, you and Aaron your brother, and tell the rock before their eyes to yield its water; so you shall bring water out of the rock for them; so you shall give drink to the congregation and their cattle."

Moses and Aaron apparently thought that the people had tried God's patience too much and doubted the mercy of God. They doubted that they should perform this task God had given them. Instead of speaking to the rock as God had commanded, Moses struck it twice. God was displeased with his lack of faith, and because of his doubt, Moses was not allowed to enter the Promised Land.

Thirty-eight years had passed, and Moses knew that the time of wandering in the wilderness was nearly over. God told him to move away from Kadesh, but not to engage in battle with the people of Edom when they passed through there. Moses was pleased to hear this news, for he was ready to leave the land of Kadesh.

He asked the king of Edom to be allowed to pass through his territory, and he promised to pay for everything the Israelites might use on their way. But the king of Edom refused. So Moses was forced to march around Edom and came to Mount Hor.

When they reached Mount Hor, the Lord commanded Moses to take Aaron and Aaron's son, Eleazar, up on the mountain and strip Aaron of his priestly robes. Then, Moses was to clothe Eleazar with them. Moses obeyed the Lord, and there on the mountaintop, after losing his priestly robes, Aaron died. When the people heard of his death, they mourned him for thirty days.

Because the king of Edom had refused passage through his land, the Israelites had to pass through the desert and the scorching Wilderness of Sin in order to enter the Promised Land. The heat there was almost unbearable. So the people again complained against Moses for having brought them out of Egypt.

"Why have you brought us up out of Egypt to die in the wilderness?" they asked. "For there is no food and no water, and we loathe this worthless food."

God punished them for this complaint by sending venomous snakes into their midst. The bite of the snakes was painful like fire and caused many to die. Moses prayed to God for the afflicted people, and God heard his prayer.

He told Moses to make a statue of one of the snakes out of bronze, and then to lift it up on a pole so the people could see it. He promised that all who saw the bronze snake, even if they had been bitten, would live. Moses obeyed, and when those who were bitten looked up at the bronze snake, their wounds were healed.

After this punishment the Israelites were more obedient. They traveled two hundred miles through the desert and entered the territory of the Amorites. Moses sent messengers to their king, asking permission to pass through his territory. Like the king of Edom, he refused, and he sent his army to meet the Israelites. A battle ensued, and the Israelites won.

After the battle, the Israelites marched forward through the land, taking possession of the Amorites' capital and many of their towns. Then they marched north and conquered the king of Bashan.

Moses divided the territory east of the Jordan that the Israelites had conquered among the tribes of Gad, Reuben, and Manasseh. These three tribes had asked for this land, but they had promised to cross the Jordan with the other Israelites to help conquer the area west of the river.

Moses knew that the time of his leadership had passed. At the advice of the Lord, he appointed Joshua, who was of the tribe of Ephraim, to lead the people. Joshua had been the faithful lieutenant of Moses. He had gone with him up the mountain when he received the first tablets of stone, and he was one of the twelve scouts sent to explore the Promised Land.

In the presence of Eleazar, the high priest, Moses placed his hands on Joshua to show that from this time forward he was the civil and military leader of the Israelites. By God's command, Eleazar was the high priest and leader in religious matters.

God told Moses the time when he was to die. After blessing the Israelites, Moses went up alone to the top of Mount Nebo. From this mountain God showed him the Promised Land sprawling in the distance.

When Moses saw it, he rejoiced. Here, at the ripe old age of one hundred and twenty years, full of gratitude to God, he died. There would never be another prophet like Moses in Israel, for no one would know God face to face the way he did, and no one would see all the signs and wonders that the Lord showed to him and him alone.

God Himself buried Moses, not the people, and no one knows the exact spot. God hid the grave of Moses from the Israelites so that they wouldn't take his body and worship it, for they were easily tempted to idolatry. The Israelites mourned for Moses for thirty days.

The Story of Balaam

Before the death of Moses, a very strange and peculiar development was taking place that the Israelites didn't know about. They were being watched by a pagan prophet and a bitter king who wanted to curse them.

This all happened before the Israelites crossed the Jordan, when Balak, king of the Moabites, sent presents to a prophet named Balaam, who lived far away in Mesopotamia. Balak begged Balaam to come and curse the people of Israel. He was fearful of their great numbers and worried about what they would do in his land. Balaam welcomed the presents delivered by the elders of the Moabites, and he invited them to lodge with him that night.

But God spoke to Balaam and said, "You shall not go with them; you shall not curse the people, for they are blessed."

So Balaam refused to go to the land of Moab with the messengers of King Balak.

But Balak was not discouraged. Again he sent messengers to Balaam, begging him to come and curse the Israelites. This time God told Balaam to go with them, but to do what He Himself commanded.

So Balaam saddled his donkey and, with two of his servants, accompanied the messengers to the land of Moab. As they went along, an angel with a drawn sword stood in their path. Balaam couldn't see him, but the donkey did, and she ran into a field to get away from the angel. Balaam beat the donkey and forced her to return to the road.

They went on a little farther and came to a place where the road cut between two huge rocks. The angel again stood in the way with a sword drawn, and again the donkey refused to go forward. When Balaam beat her, yelling for the donkey to go, she went to one side and crushed his foot against the rock.

Balaam was furious and started to beat the donkey cruelly. The poor beast fell to the ground, but then an amazing thing happened.

The donkey turned to Balaam and began to speak! God gave her the power to rebuke her master.

The animal said, "What have I done to you, that you have struck me these three times?"

Once he got over his shock, Balaam answered, "Because you have made sport of me. I wish I had a sword in my hand, for then I would kill you."

The donkey answered, "Am I not your donkey, upon which you have ridden all your life long to this day? Was I ever accustomed to do so to you?"

Balaam, knowing that the donkey had never behaved this way before, answered, "No."

Then Balaam saw the angel standing ready to kill him with the sword. He fell down on his face, and the angel said to him, "Why have your struck your donkey these three times? Behold, I have come forth to withstand you, because your way is perverse before me; and the donkey saw me, and turned aside before me these three times. If she had not turned aside from me, surely just now I would have slain you and let her live."

Balaam replied, "I have sinned, for I did not know that

you stood in the road against me. Now therefore, if it is evil in your sight, I will go back again."

The angel said to go with the men who wished to do Moses and the Israelites harm, but to speak only the words that God would instruct him to say.

When Balaam finally arrived, the king came out to meet him and brought him to a high place. Down below they could see the camp of the Israelites. It was now that Balak expected Balaam to curse the Israelites, but Balaam said, "How can I curse whom God has not cursed? How can I denounce whom the Lord has not denounced?" And instead of cursing them, Balaam blessed the Israelites three times, going against the wishes of the king.

Balak was furious at Balaam for refusing to curse the Israelites, and he sent him out of the land of Moab to return to his own country. But Balaam prophesied before he left, saying, "A star shall come forth out of Jacob, and a scepter shall rise out of Israel. . . . By Jacob shall dominion be exercised."

We should note that while a story with a talking donkey is always worth telling, the talking donkey isn't the reason why this story is important. What is most important for us to hear is the prophet Balaam's prediction that a "star shall come forth out of Jacob, and a scepter shall rise out of Israel." This prophecy foretold the coming of a great King who would be born among the descendants of Jacob. Once more, God was telling His people that one day He would send them a Savior.

CHAPTER 10

Joshua, Commander of the Israelites

The Land of Canaan

Canaan, the land God had promised to the Israelites, was located near the eastern end of the Mediterranean Sea. The coastal area of that sea, occupied by the Philistines and Phoenicians, formed the land's western edge. To the east of Canaan lay the Dead Sea and the great Eastern Desert now occupied by the nations of Syria, Jordan, and Saudi Arabia. To the north were the mountainous lands of the Phoenicians, now Lebanon. And to the south lay the Sinai Desert, a part of Egypt.

Canaan lay almost at the center of the ancient world, in the temperate zone. The Bible describes it as a land of brooks and flowing waters, whose hills and plains grew abundant wheat, barley, olives, vineyards, and fruit trees.

From north to south, it was about one hundred and fifty miles long. Its width from east to west was about eighty miles—forty miles on each side of the Jordan River. Altogether, it was about as large as the state of Maryland.

The land east of the Jordan was a great plateau two thousand feet above sea level. Three rivers, the Arnon, the Jabbok, and the Yarmuk, ran at right angles to the Jordan and divided the country into three sections.

The northern section, between the Yarmuk and the Lebanon Mountains, was a great plain, about fifty miles long and twenty miles wide. In the middle section there were forest-clad hills, rich in foliage. The third, the southern section, was bleak, with very little vegetation. The region east of the Jordan was better suited than the region to the west for the raising of flocks and herds.

Along the coast of the Mediterranean ran an unbroken plain from Gaza to Mount Carmel. This plain was about eighty miles long. In the south it was twenty miles wide, but it grew narrower to the north. It was very fertile country, though in some places the streams that ran through it created marshes.

Between this plain and the Jordan River was a plateau about twenty-five miles wide. Like the plateau on the east of the Jordan, it was more fertile in the north than in the south, where it is bleak and almost barren. However, olives grew here in abundance, as did pines and laurels, and there was a wilderness just west of the Jordan.

Going north, the land became more fertile. Here, oranges grew and forests covered the hills. Still farther north, the vegetation became even more plentiful. The hills were clothed with forests of oak, maple, and poplar, and wildflowers dotted the pastures. Here were found the Plain of Esdraelon and Mount Tabor, and four miles to the southwest a mountain called Little Hermon.

The Jordan valley extended from the foot of Mount Hermon to the southern shore of the Dead Sea. At the base of Mount Hermon this valley was a thousand feet above sea level, but by the time it reached the Dead Sea, it fell to more than a thousand feet below sea level.

Chains of mountains ran practically the whole length of the country—one to the west of the Jordan, the other to the east. West of each mountain chain was a valley: one on the coast of the Mediterranean, the other along the Jordan River.

Mount Carmel was the only mountain of importance along the coast. At its highest point, it was one thousand, seven hundred and fifty feet above sea level. Many other mountains also surrounded the area, including Mount Hebron, Mount Olivet, Mount Herbal, Mount Gerizim, Little Hermon, and Mount Tabor.

The Jordan was the most important river in the land, stretching more than two hundred and sixty miles long. At some places it was one hundred and eighty feet wide and twelve feet deep. It ran from north to south, past several lakes, and finally emptied into the Dead Sea.

There were two seasons in Canaan: the rainy season, which lasted from October to May, and the dry season, which extended through the rest of the year. The rainfall was the greatest during January and February. August was the hottest month of the year, February the coldest.

The highest temperature in the dry season was typically one hundred and ten degrees. Freezing weather was rare, though there was an occasional fall of snow. The flowers began to bloom and the trees to bud in the middle of April, about six weeks before the end of the rainy season.

The Inhabitants of Canaan
Of all the various tribes of people who lived in Canaan when Joshua led the Israelites across the Jordan, none was

more powerful than the Philistines. Scholars have disagreed about their origins, but they seem to have been one of several "sea peoples" from the area of the Aegean Sea who migrated east and joined forces to attack Egypt. The Egyptians defeated them, however, and they settled on the coast in the southern part of Canaan.

In time, they began to wage war on the tribes to the north and to the east. Their soldiers were well trained, and their weapons, made of iron instead of bronze, were superior to those of their enemies.

From the biblical name of this people, *Philistines,* the Promised Land received the name *Palestine.* They brought with them into Canaan the arts and crafts they had learned in their original homeland. They were a cultured people, but they worshiped idols. Though the Philistines would in time cause God's chosen people much trouble and suffering, they would also teach them the valuable art of working in iron.

The Phoenicians, who also lived along the coast of Canaan to the north and beyond, seem to have been the first people to develop an alphabet, with each letter representing a sound. The Israelites had brought from Egypt a knowledge of picture writing. But they soon discovered that the script used by the Phoenicians was better suited for writing down the wonderful story of how God had chosen them and protected them during their exodus from Egypt and their wanderings in the desert. Following the example of the Philistines, the Israelites eventually formed an alphabet of their own.

The Syrians were a nomadic people who had wandered from Arabia and made settlements throughout Mesopotamia. They had come as far south as Damascus, where they established a kingdom. They became very strong and later on caused the Israelites much trouble.

The Moabites, meanwhile, took their name from Moab, a son of Lot. After the destruction of Sodom and Gomorrah, he settled in the country bordering on the east coast of the Dead Sea. The territory that he chose for himself was a plateau that rose about forty-three hundred feet above the Dead Sea.

Shortly before the Israelites entered the Promised Land, the Moabites had been driven out of the northern portion of their country by the Amorites. The Moabites were hostile to the Israelites, and it was only after many years that peace was made with them.

The Edomites, descendants of Esau, lived south of the Dead Sea in the land of Moab, and were very hostile to the Israelites. They worshiped their false gods using idols on the tops of hills called "high places." They were a source of temptation to the Israelites and led many of them away from the worship of the one true God. The prophets and other holy men often preached against the Edomites and threatened them with destruction.

The Amorites were descendants of Canaan. They first dwelled west of the Jordan, but later crossed to the east and drove the Moabites out of their territory between the Jabbok and the Arnon rivers. Here they formed two kingdoms: the northern, Bashan, with Edrei its capital and Og its king; and the southern, Gilead, with Heshbon its capital, and Sihon its king. They too served as a source of temptation and bitterness for the Israelites. So God would one day allow the Israelites to destroy them, so that His people would not imitate their life of idolatry.

This overview of Canaan should help us understand better the challenges faced by the Israelites as they entered the Promised Land. The process of settlement would be difficult and would take some time. And even after they settled in, they would have to fight the temptation to adopt the wicked ways of the peoples who had been there when they came.

Joshua's Conquests

Canaan was to become the home of the Israelites after forty years of wandering in the desert. But first they had to conquer the land and drive out the inhabitants. To do so, they used various weapons—swords, spears, the bow and arrow, and slings—and for armor they had shields and helmets made of leather or bronze.

To capture a city, the Israelites would ram large wooden beams against its gates and walls. Sometimes they would dig tunnels under its walls and invade, or they would throw torches over the walls to set the city afire. At other times, they would coax the people outside the city, where they would engage them in hand-to-hand combat.

Before Joshua crossed the Jordan, he knew he needed to find out the strength of the cities they wanted to conquer. He sent two spies to Jericho and the surrounding neighborhoods. There, his spies lodged with a woman named Rahab. But before long, the spies were recognized and reported to the king.

When Rahab heard that the king was sending his soldiers after the men to arrest them, she hid them on the roof of her house. The king's soldiers sought them in vain but never found them. When the soldiers had gone, Rahab made the spies promise that when the city was taken they would spare her and her relatives. In turn, she agreed to display a scarlet cord in her window as a sign to Joshua that the city was ready to fall.

When the spies agreed to this plan, she let them down from the roof by a rope, and they fled to the mountains. Here they stayed for three days before crossing the Jordan and rejoining Joshua. The spies told Joshua there would be no trouble in conquering the city because the people were overcome by fear even at the mere thought of the attack.

After three days, at God's command, Joshua ordered the priests to carry the Ark of the Covenant into the Jordan River. As soon as they had set foot in the water, the course of the river stopped, and a dry path appeared, much as Moses had parted the Red Sea. The priests carried the Ark to the middle of the river and remained standing there until all the Israelites had passed over.

At the prompting of the Lord, Joshua then appointed one man from every tribe to return to the Jordan, and to bring back with him a large stone from the river bed. With those stones the Israelites built a monument in the middle of the river to honor their miraculous passage.

After the monument was completed, Joshua commanded the priests to carry the Ark out of the river bed. As soon as they had done so, the river began once more to take its natural course.

On the western bank of the river in the plains of Jericho, at a place called Gilgal, the Israelites pitched their camp and celebrated the Feast of the Passover. The manna that God had provided every day during their long wanderings in the desert now stopped appearing. They had food produced by the land, so they no longer needed the manna. Their wilderness journey was over.

Soon, the Israelites would invade the powerful city of Jericho. One night an angel of the Lord with a drawn sword appeared to Joshua and gave him detailed instructions about how Jericho was to be taken.

As the Lord instructed, Joshua sent forty thousand fighting men to march around the walls of the city every day for six days. On the seventh day, the soldiers, the

priests carrying the Ark of the Covenant, and all the Israelites marched around the walls seven times.

At the end of the seventh time around the city, Joshua
gave the command, "Shout, for the Lord has given you
the city."

At that moment, seven trumpets sounded a continu-
ous blast, the people gave a mighty shout, and the walls
fell! The soldiers rushed into the city from wherever they
stood and killed all the inhabitants except Rahab and her
family, who had helped their spies.

Joshua then marched against Ai, a city northwest of Jericho. The spies he sent to scout this city underestimated those they would attack, telling Joshua to only send a portion of their army. He followed their bad advice, and the inhabitants of Ai, on seeing Joshua's forces, rushed on them and defeated the Israelites.

Joshua cried out to the Lord, asking him why He had allowed the Israelites to be defeated. God revealed to Joshua that the cause of the defeat was the disobedience of one of his men. The guilty man was found to be a man named Achan, who had retained some of the treasures of Jericho for himself, though God had commanded that all the treasure be given to the Tabernacle. Achan had stolen silver and gold, then hidden it in the ground under his tent. For his crime, he was punished with death.

Once Achan had been removed from the people, God said to Joshua, "Do not fear or be dismayed; take all the fighting men with you, and arise, go up to Ai; see, I have given into your hand the king of Ai, and his people, his city, and his land."

In his second attack, Joshua resorted to strategy. He sent five thousand men to lie in ambush behind the city. With another five thousand he approached the gates. Just as before, the soldiers of Ai rushed out at them, and the Israelites, pretending to flee, tricked them into pursuing them far from the city walls. The army hiding in ambush then closed in from the rear and destroyed the city.

All the people of Canaan were now in great fear and decided to join forces. Five Amoite cities banded together to attack Joshua, with the king of Jerusalem serving as their leader. Because the city of Gibeon would not join their league but made a treaty with Joshua instead, they decided to punish it.

Joshua hurried by night to assist the city of Gibeon. He came upon the enemy's camp and attacked it by surprise. The Lord assisted by killing many of the enemy warriors with large hailstones.

Though the battle was going well, Joshua feared nightfall would come and end the battle before their victory was complete. In the dark, the armies could no longer see to fight. The combat would cease and the enemy could regroup to fight another day.

With great confidence in God, Joshua cried out to the sun and moon, commanding them to stop moving across the sky. God answered his prayer, and in that moment, the sun and moon both stood still, giving Joshua the time he needed to secure victory. The five kings fled and took refuge in a cave, but Joshua pursued them and killed them all. By this and other victories he gained control of the southern half of Canaan.

The cities in the north of Canaan also attempted to unite their forces against Joshua. But God was with him and the Israelite armies that he led. He marched against these enemies and defeated them as well. He followed them as they fled to ensure they were all destroyed, then returned and took their cities for the Israelites.

Joshua's Last Days

After this third military campaign, Joshua divided the land west of the Jordan among the tribes. According to the Law, certain cities and their surrounding areas in each of the tribal lands were given to the priests and the Levites. The three tribes whose land was across the river went back to the east shore of the Jordan, receiving Joshua's blessing before they left. He also warned them and the other tribes of the danger of falling into idolatry.

Joshua had been God's faithful and obedient servant all his life. He was a great military commander, leading soldiers to victory in every battle. Now he divided the spoils among them and settled down to a peaceful life at Timnath-serah for the rest of his days.

Joshua assembled the people at Shechem and urged them to observe the Law and to avoid idolatry. Then he died at the age of one hundred and ten years. Eleazar also died shortly afterwards and was succeeded as high priest by his son, Phinehas. The remains of their ancestor Joseph, which the people had brought with them from Egypt, were buried at Shechem, in Jacob's field.

Joseph's descendants, under Joshua's leadership, had become victorious in Canaan. Today, as Christians we pray often for peace in the world, so it may be difficult to understand why the Lord wanted the Israelites to fight and defeat the peoples who lived in Canaan. Perhaps if we could go back in time and witness the great evils practiced by those peoples, we might better understand God's plan.

In any case, God made a way for the Israelites to settle in the land He had promised to give them. But as we will see, things did not always go well in their new home.

CHAPTER 11

The Israelites in the Promised Land

The Time of the Judges

When the Israelites took possession of their new country, they adopted a simple way of life. They didn't have one king or ruler over all the people. Instead, each tribe or family was independent and had its own head.

The Israelites began to enjoy a life of ease and prosperity. They preferred this life to the hardships and dangers of war that they had endured for so many years. But too much of the easy life weakened their bodies and spirits.

Many of the Israelites forgot how hard they had worked to achieve their prosperity, and they became lazy. Some of them even married their pagan neighbors and in time worshipped idols themselves. The people forgot that God had commanded them to conquer all the territory and to drive out the pagan inhabitants.

God chastised the Israelites from time to time by permitting their enemies to make war against them. Their principal adversaries were the Philistines, the Moabites, the Hittites, the Midianites, the Ammonites, and the Canaanites who hadn't been conquered. The leaders of the Israelites during these times were men who kept their bodies strong through hard discipline and lots of work. When a village was threatened, they stirred up the people and led them into battle against their enemy.

When several tribes had a common enemy, they often chose, under the direction of God, one man to lead their armies. This leader was usually the man who showed the greatest strength and courage, and who could make the other leaders obey him. Such a military leader was called a *judge*.

Usually, judges had the power to rule only during the time of trouble. When the trouble was over, their power was taken away from them and given back to the heads of the tribes.

The Israelites were ruled by a number of judges throughout several centuries. The Bible gives the names of fifteen judges. The most famous of them were Deborah, Gideon, Samson, and Samuel.

Deborah stands out as the only woman noted in the Bible to have served the Israelite people as a judge. She was a prophet as well. The people trusted her wisdom, so they brought their disputes to her to be settled.

When a Canaanite king came to power and began oppressing the Israelites, God spoke through Deborah to a man named Barak, calling him to lead an army against the Canaanites. He refused to do so unless Deborah joined him in the task. She agreed, and the Canaanite king, his general, and his forces were defeated by the army that Barak led.

Gideon Saves the Israelites

Gideon first became a hero because he had dared to over-throw the altar his father had built to the false god Baal. After destroying it, he erected an altar to the true God in its place. For this reason he was respected by the people as an honorable man of God.

Many of the people had forgotten the Lord and were worshipping the false gods of their neighbors. Because of their sins, the Lord allowed the Midianites to make war on the Israelites for seven years. These people ruined the territory belonging to the tribe of Gad and crossed the Jordan River to settle in the valleys that belonged to the tribes of Issachar and Manasseh.

There the Midianites pitched their tents and destroyed the fields of the Israelites. The Israelites were humbled by the destruction that was brought on them. So they cried to the Lord for help against this enemy.

God heard their cries and sent an angel to Gideon, who was working in the fields. The angel of the Lord said to him, "The Lord is with you, you mighty man of valor."

"If the Lord is with us," Gideon replied, "why then has all this befallen us? And where are all his wonderful deeds which our fathers recounted to us? . . . The Lord has cast us off, and given us into the hand of Midian."

God told Gideon that he was to lead His chosen people against the invaders. The Lord promised to be with him and to give him victory. But Gideon wanted a sign from the Lord to guarantee what He promised.

Gideon told God that he would place a woolen fleece on the threshing floor, where the grain was beaten to sep-arate the kernels from the chaff. When Gideon returned the next morning, this would be the sign that God would do as He promised: There would be dew on the fleece, but not anywhere else on the ground.

The next morning, Gideon woke up and found the fleece covered in dew, so much that when he wrung it, he filled a whole bowl full of water. But the ground all around was dry.

Still, Gideon was not convinced. He asked God for another sign, the very opposite of the first. This time, he asked for the dew to cover the ground while the fleece remained dry.

God did as Gideon asked. The next morning, the ground around the fleece was wet, while the fleece remained dry.

Full of confidence, Gideon set out to raise an army to protect the Israelites. In a short time he gathered about thirty-two thousand men. But in case the Israelites were tempted to trust too much in their own strength and forget that God was their Deliverer, the Lord told Gideon to choose from among them only three hundred men for the task.

First, Gideon persuaded twenty-two thousand men to return home. These were men who were probably less motivated to fight than the others, since they were easily convinced to leave.

The remaining ten thousand men he ordered to drink from the river. At the command of God he watched to see which way they drank the water. He was to choose those who gathered up the water in their hands and drank it from their palms. Whoever drank this way showed that even while they were drinking, they were keeping their heads up, alert to watch for the enemy.

There were three hundred such men. With these three hundred men, Gideon descended one night into the Valley of Esdraelon, where the Midianites and their allies were asleep in their tents. He divided his force into three companies and stationed them at different points around the enemy.

Every one of Gideon's soldiers had a trumpet and a pitcher in which he carried a lamp. At midnight, Gideon blew his trumpet as a signal. The three hundred also blew their trumpets, broke their pitchers, showed their lamps, and shouted, "A sword for the Lord and for Gideon!"

So great was the noise that the Midianites thought they were surrounded by a powerful army. So they fled away, fighting and killing one another in their panic. Gideon pursued them until the last of them was dead.

At this time, the Israelites began to say among themselves that it would be better for them if they had a king to rule over them. After all, the nations around them all had kings. And even though there was much jealousy among the different tribes, they thought that a king would unite them and make it possible for them to conquer their enemies once and for all, bringing back peace to the land.

Thinking this way, the Israelites forgot that God was their King and that, if they were faithful to Him, they would be a united people. They tried to make Gideon their king. But he said to them, "I will not rule over you, and my son will not rule over you; the Lord will rule over you."

For forty years, the people had peace. Then Gideon died and was buried in his father's tomb. But the time would come when Israel needed a new judge to defend them from their enemies. This time, God was sending someone with astounding physical strength.

The Origins of Samson
After the death of Gideon, the Israelites again fell into idol worship. They neglected to go and worship at Shiloh, where the Tabernacle was located, on the great feasts. So God chastised them by allowing the Philistines to become their enemies.

For forty years the Philistines waged war against them. They invaded the territory of the Israelites and took possession of the cities that belonged to the tribes of Judah, Dan, and Benjamin.

During the time of the Philistine troubles, a boy named Samson was born at Zorah. An angel had foretold his birth to his mother. Up until that time, she had not been able to have children. The angel had commanded the parents to separate the boy from others for a special purpose. His hair was not to be cut, nor was he to drink wine or other strong drink.

Samson was dedicated by his parents to the service of God, who had destined him to be a scourge to the Philistines. Unlike the other judges, he had no army, but depended instead on his own tremendous strength. He was so strong that once, when he was a small boy and a young lion attacked him, he seized it in both hands and tore it apart!

Samson Against the Philistines

After Samson grew up, he began his campaign against the Philistines in a strange way. He caught three hundred foxes and tied their tails together, then fastened lighted torches to them. He set the foxes loose in the fields of the Philistines so they would run rampant and set the crops ablaze.

All the corn in the fields, all the grapes in the vineyards, and all the olives on the trees were burned. In retaliation, the Philistines burned his father-in-law's house, and Samson's wife perished in the flames. Samson was furious and went into the city nearby. He slaughtered a large number of the inhabitants before fleeing into the territory of the tribe of Judah.

The Philistines sent an army after him. Though Samson was attempting to avoid capture, the men of Judah, fearing the Philistines, bound Samson and brought him to the enemy. When Samson was brought into the camp of the Philistines, he broke the cords that bound him, took the jawbone of a donkey that he found lying on the ground, and used it to kill a thousand Philistines. The rest fled in fear.

On another occasion Samson slept in Gaza, a Philistine city. The Philistine guards surrounded the city and closed the gates so that he couldn't escape. But he rose up, took the gates of the city with their posts and bolts, put them on his shoulders, and carried them to the top of a neighboring hill. It seemed there was nothing the Philistines could do to capture and kill Samson—until Samson fell in love.

The woman's name was Delilah, and she was a Philistine from the valley of Sorek. The Philistines, seeing that Samson was so taken by her, approached Delilah and said, "Entice him, and see wherein his great strength lies, and by what means we may overpower him, that we may bind him to subdue him; and we will each give you eleven hundred pieces of silver."

Delilah accepted the bribe. She went to Samson and asked what was the source of his great strength. At first, Samson resisted, telling her lies and tricking her into thinking the wrong thing about where his strength came from. But eventually he relented and confessed that the source of his strength lay in his long hair.

"A razor has never come upon my head. . . . If I be shaved, then my strength will leave me, and I shall become weak, and be like any other man."

So at night while he was asleep, Delilah cut his hair and called in the soldiers to capture him. The woman he loved had betrayed him. The soldiers were able to control him, for his strength had faded. They blinded him and cast him into a prison in the city of Gaza.

But in the darkness of the dungeon, Samson's hair began to grow back.

One day a great feast was held in the city. Several thousand people were gathered in the banquet hall. Samson was brought from the prison so that the guests might amuse themselves by making fun of him. What they didn't realize was that his hair had grown long once again.

A boy was leading the blind prisoner into the hall. Samson asked the boy to lead him toward the pillars so he could lean against them and rest. These were the same pillars that supported the roof of the great hall.

The boy led him to the pillars. Then, calling on the Lord to restore his strength, Samson took both pillars in his hands and shook them. The house fell and many were killed, including several princes of the Philistines. But Samson also perished.

The Origins of Samuel

One day, when Eli, the high priest, was sitting before the door of the Tabernacle in Shiloh, a woman approached and knelt down, praying fervently to the Lord. Her name was Hannah, and she was the wife of Elkanah.

Hannah was the second of two wives for Elkanah. The other wife had many children, but Hannah had none, so she was greatly troubled. To make matters worse, the other wife would tease and mock Hannah because she was childless.

As Hannah prayed, she began to weep as though her heart would break. She made a vow, saying, "O Lord of hosts, if You will indeed look on the affliction of Your maidservant, and remember me, and not forget Your maidservant, but will give to Your maidservant a son, then I will give him to the Lord all the days of his life."

Eli thought she was drunk and was making a mockery of the sacred Tabernacle. But Hannah defended herself, saying, "No, my lord, I am a woman sorely troubled; I have drunk neither wine nor strong drink, but I have been pouring out my soul before the Lord."

Eli responded, "Go in peace, and the God of Israel grant your petition which you have made to him."

Hannah returned to her home, and the day came when God answered her prayer, and she bore a son. While he was still an infant, his parents took him to Shiloh and offered him to Eli, the high priest. Hannah reminded Eli who she was and how they had met that day in the Tabernacle. She renewed her pledge to offer up her son to God.

Then Elkanah and Hannah returned home, but the child was left behind in the care of the high priest. He was called Samuel, and he grew up in the Tabernacle. He learned all about the religious services performed there and how to serve Eli.

Among the priests who took part in the worship in the Tabernacle were the two sons of Eli, whose names were Hophni and Phinehas. They were wicked men, robbing people who came to the Tabernacle to offer sacrifices. They used their holy office to make themselves rich.

Eli knew of the wickedness of his sons, but though he disciplined them from time to time, he didn't drive them out of the Tabernacle and punish them as they deserved to be punished. For this reason, God was displeased with Eli.

Samuel Speaks to the Lord

One night, while Eli and Samuel were sleeping in the Tabernacle, the boy heard a voice.

"Samuel! Samuel!"

It was the Lord calling out to him, but Samuel thought it was Eli. He ran over to Eli and said, "Here I am, for you called me."

"I did not call," Eli replied, "lie down again."

A moment later, the Lord called again. "Samuel!"

He rose again and approached Eli, but Eli said, "I did not call, my son; lie down again."

Eli sent him back to bed, and a third time the Lord called out, and a third time Samuel came to Eli. "Here I am, for you called me."

Eli finally understood it was the Lord calling the boy. He said, "Go, lie down; and if he calls you, you shall say, 'Speak, Lord, for Your servant hears.'"

So Samuel returned, and when he heard the voice again calling his name, he said, "Speak, for Your servant hears."

Then the Lord spoke to Samuel. He told him about the punishment He was about to inflict on Eli's sons for their sins. In addition, Eli himself would be punished for neglecting to discipline his sons.

The next day Eli asked Samuel what the Lord had said to him. Samuel reported all that he had heard. He didn't hide anything about the punishment that was to fall on Eli and his sons.

Samuel eventually grew to manhood, and during that time the Philistines had stolen more and more land away from the Israelites. In despair, the Israelites sent to Shiloh for the Ark of the Covenant. They hoped that by carrying the Ark into battle they might gain victory over the Philistines, for then God would be with them.

The Ark was brought to them, and the two sons of Eli went with it. The eruption of shouts and cheers from the soldiers when they saw the Ark frightened the Philistines for a time. They had heard that the Ark of Israel's God had come into the camp, and they knew what He had done to the Egyptians so many years before. But they soon gathered their courage and attacked the Israelites, defeating them once more.

The two sons of Eli were killed in this battle, and the Ark of the Covenant was captured by the Philistines. This news was brought to Eli, who was now old and blind. When he heard it, he fell from his chair and died.

The two sons were killed for their crimes, and the father died because of his failure to correct them. The prophecy uttered to Samuel that night in the Tabernacle had been fulfilled.

Samuel Against the Philistines

The Philistines took the Ark of the Covenant to Ash-
dod, one of their cities near the sea. They placed it in
the temple of their god, Dagon. The next day they found
the statue of Dagon on its face before the Ark. They set
it up again, but the next morning it was found again
on the ground, with the head and hands of the idol
broken off.

The city was then plagued with mice, and many of
their people died. So the chiefs of the Philistines decided
to move the Ark from one city to another, but the people
of all the cities where the Ark was taken were afflicted
with painful tumors and boils. One city, Ekron, wouldn't
even allow the Ark to be placed within its walls for fear of
what would happen to them.

After several months, the Philistines decided to return
the Ark to the Israelites. They placed it on a cart and laid
beside it ten vessels of gold as an offering to take away the
guilt of their crime. Two oxen were hitched to the cart,
but without a guide to steer them.

The oxen left the city of Ekron and carried the Ark
north to Bethshemesh. Here, they stopped in the fields of
a priest. The priest broke up the wood of the cart and, piling it on a stone in his field, offered the oxen as a sacrifice
of thanksgiving for the return of the Ark to the Israelites.

Some of the people of Bethshemesh, prompted by cu-
riosity, raised the coverings of the Ark to look inside it.
Seventy of them died because of this act of irreverence.
The rest were frightened, so they sent the Ark on to another city, one known for its holiness.

The attacks of Samson and the punishments that followed the capture of the Ark had put fear into the hearts
of the Philistines. Samuel wanted to take advantage of
this fear and believed it was time to wage war against

them. He preached to the people and urged them to return to the worship of God.

"If you are returning to the Lord with all your heart, then put away the foreign gods . . . and direct your heart to the Lord, and serve Him only, and He will deliver you out of the hand of the Philistines."

Samuel inspired the people to return to the Lord. He gathered an army at Mizpah and offered a sacrifice to God to obtain victory over the Philistines. While the sacrifice was being offered, the Philistines began their attack. But God was with Samuel. He terrified the Philistines with a terrible storm, throwing them into a state of confusion.

And so it was, with help from the Lord, that Samuel was able to defeat the Philistines.

The Story of Ruth

While the judges were ruling, a famine swept over the land. A man by the name of Elimelech, who lived at Bethlehem in the territory given to the tribe of Judah, went to the country of Moab with his wife, Naomi, and his two sons. They all went in search of food.

Coming to the land of Moab, they stayed a long while, and Elimelech eventually died there, leaving Naomi alone with her two sons. The sons went on to marry Moabite women, one named Orpah, and the other named Ruth. For ten years they all dwelt together happily, but then the two sons died.

Naomi heard that God had given bread to His people in Judah, so she set out with her two daughters-in-law to return home. After they had gone a short distance, Naomi said to her daughters-in-law: "Go, return each of you to her mother's house. May the Lord deal kindly with you, as you have dealt with the dead and with me.

The Lord grant that you may find a home, each of you in the house of her husband!"

Orpah and Ruth replied, "No, we will return with you to your people."

But Naomi insisted. She told them that she had nothing to offer them, for her people were poor, and that they should go in search of husbands among their own people, the Moabites.

Finally Orpah kissed her mother-in-law and went back. But Ruth stayed.

She said, "Entreat me not to leave you or to return from following you; for where you go I will go, and where you lodge I will lodge; your people shall be my people, and your God my God; where you die I will die, and there will I be buried. May the Lord do so to me and more also if even death parts me from you."

Naomi finally understood that Ruth was determined to go with her. They walked along together until they came to Bethlehem.

They arrived at the beginning of the barley harvest. The Law of Moses instructed those who owned fields to go through them reaping only once each year. They were not to go over the fields a second time, looking for what had been missed. Instead, any grain left on the ground was to be left there for the poor to gather for themselves.

Naomi knew a relative of her husband, a wealthy man named Boaz. He had rich fields of barley. Ruth asked permission from Naomi to go into the field to gather after the reapers of Boaz, and Naomi agreed.

So Ruth went into the fields and followed the reapers of Boaz. She worked hard all day, gathering what they left behind, without taking even a moment to rest. Boaz took note of her and asked who she was.

"It is the Moabite maiden," his servant replied, "who came back with Naomi from the country of Moab."

Boaz had heard of the great kindness Ruth had shown to her mother-in-law, and he was very pleased to see her working in his field. He told her that he would protect her and see that no harm should befall her, and he took care that she was given something to eat at noon.

As the days went on, Boaz came to love Ruth very dearly. He married her and placed her in charge of his house, making a home for Naomi as well.

Later, Boaz and Ruth had a son named Obed. Their son would one day become the grandfather of David the king, and through his family would come the Savior of the world.

We've learned about many great figures of the Old Testament, some of them wealthy, powerful, and famous in their day. But God knew that even poor, powerless, and unknown people could have a role in Israel's destiny as a nation. Such a person was Ruth.

Her story seems tiny and insignificant compared to the colossal figures of the Bible. But this poor and humble widow, who was not even born an Israelite, would make her mark on the future of Israel and the whole world. For through her great-grandson, a royal line of descendants would lead directly to the Savior of the human race. What a lesson she can teach us that even small acts of kindness can lead to the grandest of results!

PART FOUR
How God's Chosen People Lived Under Their Kings

CHAPTER 12

Saul and David

Israel Cries Out for a King

The Israelites were not content with the rule of the judges. They longed to be united under one leader, a king, like the other nations around them. In the time of Samuel, the people became restless and insisted that he appoint a king to rule over them.

In vain, Samuel reminded them that God was their King. But they wouldn't listen to him. They wanted a human king to lead them to a final victory over the Canaanites and the Philistines. They thought a human king would prevent civil war and stop them from robbing one another, while he kept the neighboring enemies at a distance. Moreover, though Samuel was a good judge and governed them well, they were afraid that his sons, who were weak men, would not continue in the footsteps of their father.

Samuel tried to reason with them. He showed them that they would have to suffer the hardships of taxation for the support of a king and soldiers to supply an army. In order to be a united nation, they need only obey God's command to worship only at the Tabernacle as the Law of Moses commanded. If their neighbors made war on them, it was a punishment for their sins and, above all, for their failure to worship at the Tabernacle.

Samuel urged them to give up their desire for a king and promised them that the wars would come to an end. By seeking to have a king, they were sinning against the will of God.

The people didn't listen to Samuel. They prayed to God, begging Him for a king. Finally, God yielded to their desires, saying to Samuel, "Listen to their voice, and make them a king."

To bring them back to true worship and prevent them from worshiping false gods, God gave them a human king. He promised them that they would be a great nation under their king as long as they were faithful to Him.

Even so, the day would come when the Israelites would realize the difference between the cruel tyranny of human kings and the kind and merciful guidance of the divine King.

Samuel Anoints Saul

The man God chose to be the first king of the Israelites belonged to the tribe of Benjamin. His name was Saul, and he lived in the city of Gibeah. Saul was a tall and handsome man. He was well respected and even admired.

One day, Saul was searching for some of his father's donkeys that had wandered away. He and a servant searched far and wide looking for the lost animals. When they came to the land of Zuph, Saul reasoned that they had searched all they could, and they should return home. But his servant claimed there was a holy man of God in the nearby city, and he would be able to help them locate the lost donkeys. That holy man was Samuel.

They went and found Samuel at the gates of the city. As soon as Samuel saw Saul, he recalled a message from the Lord the day before:

"Tomorrow about this time I will send to you a man from the land of Benjamin, and you shall anoint him to be prince over my people Israel. He shall save my people . . . because their cry has come to me."

Samuel knew this was the man God had spoken about. He took Saul and his servant into his house and gave them a place at the head of all the guests. He gave them the best portions of meat that he had set apart for the man whom the Lord would send that day. Saul ate with Samuel and slept in his house that night.

The next day, at dawn, Samuel called Saul and they went out together, along with Saul's servant. As they approached the edge of the city, Samuel said to Saul, "Tell the servant to pass on before us, and when he has passed on stop here yourself for a while, that I may make known to you the word of God."

When Samuel was alone with Saul, having sent the servant forward, he poured oil on his head. He kissed him and said, "Has not the Lord anointed you to be prince over his people Israel? And you shall reign over the people of the Lord and you will save them from the hand of their enemies."

Samuel also told Saul that after departing, he would come across two men by Rachel's tomb. They would tell him that the lost donkeys he sought were found, but that his father no longer cares about the donkeys, having become anxious about his son instead. Then Samuel told Saul he would encounter other men: some who would give him bread and wine as gifts, then several prophets who would play instruments. Saul would prophesy with them about things to come.

Samuel declared that after all these unusual meetings, the Spirit of the Lord would come on Saul and be with him. After leaving Samuel, Saul was given a new heart by the Lord, and all these signs came to pass.

When Saul returned to Gibeah, his father asked him where he had been. Saul said that he had been in search of the lost animals, and on his way he had met Samuel. But Saul didn't tell his father how Samuel had anointed him king. He waited for Samuel to reveal God's choice.

Not long after Saul's anointing, Samuel gathered together the twelve tribes of the Israelites at Mizpah, near Gibeah, and told them that God had chosen a king from among them. But they would have to discover him by casting lots. They would pool together candidates from the tribes and select him that way.

They cast lots, and Saul was chosen. In vain, they looked for him among the crowd, but he wasn't there.

Then the Lord spoke and said, "Behold, he has hidden himself."

They ran and found Saul, bringing him back to the place where all the people were gathered. Among the people, Saul stood high above them, being the tallest by some margin.

Samuel said to the people, "Do you see him whom the Lord has chosen? There is none like him among all the people."

And the people shouted, "Long live the king!"

Saul as King

Soon after Saul was anointed king, the Ammonites attacked the city of Jabesh-gilead. The city was about to surrender, when the people thought of their new king and sent messengers to him.

The messengers found Saul working in the field. He cut up the oxen with which he was plowing and sent a portion of the meat to every tribe. He warned that what had happened to the oxen would happen to the oxen of every tribe who refused to follow him and Samuel into war against the Ammonites. Through this warning to the people, he gathered an army for the protection of Israel.

An immense number of Israelites answered this call to battle, and Jabesh-gilead was saved. The Ammonites were defeated and driven back to their own territory.

The Israelites rejoiced over their victory. Saul was recognized everywhere as king, and they threatened anyone who opposed him with death. Saul was now a great man in the eyes of the people, just as Gideon had been after defeating the Midianites.

Samuel and Saul assembled the people at Gilgal. There, Saul was formally anointed king of the Israelites.

In the latter days of Samuel, when his sons were governing Israel, the Philistines had begun to move across the land of Judah. Saul sent his son, Jonathan, with an army of one thousand men to attack them at Gibeah, where the Philistines had a camp. Jonathan was successful in the attack and drove them out of their camp.

But the Philistines then poured into the country in greater numbers. The Israelites were so frightened that they fled.

When Saul saw his soldiers deserting him, some fleeing across the Jordan and others joining the Philistines, he became impatient. He wanted to begin the battle. But

Samuel had ordered him not to begin until he could come and offer a sacrifice, for Samuel was the only one who was authorized to perform such an act. Nevertheless, Saul, in his impatience, disobeyed Samuel and offered a sacrifice himself.

Samuel arrived a few hours later and rebuked Saul for his impatience. He foretold that the kingship would pass from Saul's family because of this act of disobedience.

Saul had displeased God, but God led him to many victories for the sake of the Israelites. A man named Abner was captain of Saul's army. He, along with Jonathan, trained the army, and with it Saul drove back his enemies: the Moabites, the Ammonites, and the Syrians.

Meanwhile, the Amalekites were harassing the Israelites in the south. God sent Saul to make war on them in their own country and to destroy them and their possessions. Saul won a great victory over the Amalekites, but he didn't obey God completely. He took the best of their flocks and treasures for himself and spared their king, in spite of God's command.

Samuel again rebuked Saul for his disobedience, but Saul laid the blame on the people. He was willing to offer the plunder in sacrifice, but God had not asked for sacrifice. He had asked for obedience.

Samuel said, "Has the Lord as great delight in burnt offerings and sacrifices, as in obeying the voice of the Lord? Behold, to obey is better to sacrifice. . . . Because you have rejected the word of the Lord, He has also rejected you from being king."

This was a warning from Samuel: Because of Saul's disobedience, the throne would pass to someone else.

Saul's story begins with great promise and excitement. He was destined by God to be the first king of the Israelites, and anointed by the holy man Samuel. But it seems that this new-found power went to his head, for not long after being anointed, he disobeyed the commands of God. This disobedience would surely cost him, as we will see. Soon, a new king, greater than he, would rise up in his place.

The Origins of David

God sent Samuel to Bethlehem to find and anoint the man who would succeed Saul as king. But Samuel was afraid Saul would discover the reason for this trip, and kill him. So God told Samuel to announce that he had come to offer a sacrifice, and when he did, God would reveal his choice for the new king.

Samuel followed the Lord's instructions. He came to the home of a man named Jesse and called him and his sons to the sacrifice. After the sacrifice, Samuel asked Jesse whether all his sons were present. All were there but the youngest, David, who was in the fields tending the flocks. At Samuel's request, David was brought to him.

When David came in, Samuel saw that he was handsome and noble-looking. The Lord told Samuel that this young man was his choice for king. So Samuel took a horn of oil and anointed David in the presence of his family, and the Spirit of the Lord came on David from that day forward.

About this time, Saul had a royal palace built for himself and for his four sons and two daughters. But neither the palace, nor the many victories he had won, could make Saul happy. Because of the warning from Samuel following his disobedience, Saul knew that the kingly office would pass from his family, and he became sad and distressed.

One day, Saul heard there was a young man at Bethlehem who was talented at playing the harp. This young harpist was David. Saul sent for David to entertain him and cheer him up. When Saul saw David and heard the sweet music he played on the harp, he was pleased and made him his armor-bearer. But he did this without knowing that David had been anointed to succeed him as king.

David Slays Goliath

Again the Philistines sent their army to attack Saul, so the Israelites went out to meet them in the Valley of Elah. The Philistines stood on a mountain on one side of the valley, while the Israelites stood on a mountain opposite them.

A man named Goliath came out from the camp of the Philistines. He was a giant, over nine feet tall and weighing hundreds of pounds. He wore a helmet and thick armor made of bronze, and he wielded a large spear.

Goliath came into the valley and cried out, "Why have you come out to draw up for battle? Am I not a Philistine, and are you not servants of Saul? Choose a man for yourselves, and let him come down to me. If he is able to fight with me and kill me, then we will be your servants; but if I prevail against him and kill him, then you shall be our servants and serve us."

When Saul and his army saw Goliath and heard his challenge, they were terrified. No soldier was brave enough to fight Goliath, even though Saul had offered his daughter in marriage to anyone who would slay him.

At this time, David's father sent him to the camp with food for his brothers stationed there with the king's army. While David was there, Goliath came out into the valley between the camps and repeated his challenge. David quickly decided that he would fight Goliath. He told his brothers this, and they laughed at him. His oldest brother

was even angry, thinking it was pride that led David to think he could kill Goliath.

But David persisted. He approached Saul and said: "Let no man's heart fail because of him; your servant will go and fight with this Philistine."

"You are not able to go against this Philistine to fight with him," Saul replied, "for you are but a youth, and he has been a man of war from his youth."

"Your servant used to keep sheep for his father," David replied; "and when there came a lion, or a bear, and took a lamb from the flock, I went after him and struck him and delivered it out of his mouth. . . . Your servant has killed both lions and bears; and this uncircumcised Philistine shall be like one of them, seeing he has defied the armies of the living God. . . . The Lord who delivered me from the paw of the lion and from the paw of the bear will deliver me from the hand of this Philistine."

So Saul said to David, "Go, and the Lord be with you." Then he placed his own helmet and armor on David.

But David said, "I cannot go with these; for I am not used to them." David took off Saul's helmet and armor. Instead, he took a sling and five smooth stones, and he went out to meet the Philistine giant.

When Goliath saw David, such a tiny boy compared to his own massive stature, he laughed and cursed him. "Come to me," he shouted, "and I will give your flesh to the birds of the air and to the beasts of the field."

David answered the Philistine: "You come to me with a sword and with a spear and with a javelin; but I come to you in the name of the Lord of hosts, the God of the armies of Israel, whom you have defied.

"This day the Lord will deliver you into my hand, and I will strike you down, and cut off your head; and I will give the dead bodies of the host of the Philistines this day to the birds of the air and to the wild beasts of the earth; that all the earth may know that there is a God in Israel, and that all this assembly may know that the Lord saves not with the sword and spear; for the battle is the Lord's and He will give you into our hand."

David then took his sling and whirled a stone at Goliath, striking him directly between the eyes and sending him tumbling to the ground. David ran up to the stunned giant, took his sword, and cut off his head.

The rest of the Philistines were shocked at the outcome of the battle. They fled in terror. The Israelites pursued and killed many of them. When they returned from the pursuit, they sang the praises of David, who was now the nation's hero. Saul then became jealous of David for the praise he received.

Even so, Saul insisted that David come live with the royal family in the palace. There, David became great friends with Saul's son, Jonathan, a noble young prince who sought in every way to do the will of God. Jonathan and David came to love each other like brothers.

The two young men swore that they would always be loyal to each other. One day, as a sign of undying friendship, Jonathan took off his royal garments and his sword, bow, and belt, and gave them to David.

Saul Persecutes David

One day Saul sat in his room in the palace, gloomy as usual, his mind filled with dark thoughts. David was summoned to play soothing music on his harp, but Saul wouldn't even look at him. He was still bitter that David's reputation on the battlefield was greater than his own.

Suddenly, in a fit of rage, Saul took a spear and threw it at David. David dodged the assault and ran from the room.

After this, Saul couldn't bear to have David in his presence. He feared him because he knew that the Lord was with him. So he gave him a thousand men and sent him on an expedition against the Philistines, hoping that he might be killed in battle. Saul told David that if he brought back proof that he had killed a hundred men, he would give him his daughter, Merab, in marriage.

As it was, David loved Michal, the younger daughter of Saul and the sister of Merab. But he accepted the condition of the king. Going out to battle, he killed two hundred Philistines. Meanwhile, the king had given Merab in marriage to someone else.

When David returned from war, Saul offered him Michal instead. David was thrilled, for he and Michal loved each other dearly. They were married amid the rejoicing of the people.

Now that David was his son-in-law, Saul's hatred of him grew more and more. He even told his servants and his son, Jonathan, about his desire to get rid of David. Jonathan, still having a deep sense of love and loyalty to David, secretly warned his friend to flee.

Again David went out and fought against the Philistines, and again he was victorious. He defeated them with a great slaughter, and they fled from his army. He returned to Saul, and once more the jealous king tried to kill him with a spear. But David escaped into the darkness of the night, fleeing to his own house.

Saul sent soldiers to watch over David's house, commanding them to kill him as soon as he came back out in the morning. When Michal learned about her father's command, she warned to husband to flee for his life. Then she secretly let him down from a window, and he escaped.

Next, Michal took a life-sized statue of a man, laid it on the bed, placed a hairy goat skin at its head, and covered it with David's clothes. In the morning, the officers of the king came to arrest David, but she told them that her husband was sick in bed.

When they reported this to Saul, he sent them back with orders to bring David to him so that he could kill him. When the soldiers came into the room, they discovered the trick Michal had played on them. Instead of David, they found the statue in bed, with the goat skin at its head.

Because Saul was out to kill him, David now became a fugitive, wandering from place to place with a band of four hundred men. At times he would take refuge in the forests. But whenever he heard that the Philistines were about to attack the Israelites, he left his hiding place to help his people.

God was with David, and he was almost always victorious. But each new victory for David only increased Saul's envy of him. Saul was determined that David must die.

David Spares Saul

Saul chased after David into the desert on the shore of the Dead Sea. When David and his men saw the king coming, they hid in a cave. Night came, and Saul, not knowing that David and his men were there, went into the very same cave to sleep. While the king slept, David's men urged him to kill the king.

They said: "Here is the day of which the Lord said to you, 'Behold, I will give your enemy into your hand, and you shall do to him as it shall seem good to you.'" But instead, David secretly crept up on Saul with his sword and cut off a piece of Saul's robe.

The next morning, Saul awoke and left the cave. When he had gone a short distance, he heard a voice calling, "My lord the king!" He turned around and saw David standing at the mouth of the cave, holding up the piece of cloth he had cut from Saul's robe.

Seeing this, Saul's heart was troubled. He knew that David could have killed him while he slept, but David chose to spare him. For a while, Saul stopped hating David, because David had shown him mercy. But David still didn't trust the king. He continued to lead a wandering life, accompanied by his faithful band of soldiers.

Saul soon forgot how David had spared his life. He set out once more to pursue and kill him. This time the king sought him in the desert of Ziph, but as the day wore on and the search proved fruitless, he and his men had to stop and rest for the night.

David sent out spies to locate Saul's camp. They entered it when Saul and his men had all fallen asleep. No one was on guard to challenge them. Again, David's men encouraged him to kill Saul.

But David replied: "Do not destroy him; for who can put forth his hand against the Lord's anointed, and be guiltless? . . . As the Lord lives, the Lord will strike him; or his day shall come to die; or he shall go down into battle and perish."

Instead of killing Saul, David crept into his tent secretly and took his spear and a cup of water from the king's side. No one from Saul's camp heard or saw him.

Going off some distance from the camp, David called out to Abner, Saul's general, by name. Abner awoke, answering, "Who are you that calls to the king?"

"Why . . . have you not kept watch over your lord the king?" David asked, showing him the items he had taken from Saul as he slept. "Now see where the king's spear is, and the jar of water that was at his head."

Saul awoke and recognized the voice calling out to them from afar.

"Is this your voice, my son David?"

David answered: "It is my voice, my lord, O king. . . . Why does my lord pursue after his servant? For what have I done? What guilt is on my hands?"

When Saul realized that David had again spared his life, he was filled with shame and said, "I have done wrong; return, my son David, for I will no more do you harm, because my life was precious in your eyes this day."

But David knew how easy it was for Saul to change his mind. So he sent back the king's spear and went on his way, while Saul returned to his palace.

It was about this time that the prophet Samuel died. He was mourned by all the people and was buried in Ramah.

Saul's Last Days

The Philistines gathered together their armies to wage a new war on the Israelites. They camped in Shunem, and Saul assembled his force at Gilboa. When Saul saw how great were the forces of the Philistines, he became afraid and asked the Lord to tell him what to do. But God did not answer him, either by dreams, or by priests, or by prophets.

After the death of Samuel, Saul had driven all the magicians and fortunetellers out of the land. So he said to his servants, "Seek out for me a woman who is a medium"—that is, a witch—"that I may go to her and inquire of her."

The servants answered, "There is a medium at Endor."

Saul disguised himself and took two men with him to consult this witch of Endor. She claimed that she could summon spirits of the dead. By night, Saul went and asked her to call on a spirit for him.

At first the woman refused. She told them that Saul had driven out all the witches of the land. She accused them of being agents of the king who had come to entrap her.

The medium didn't know she was speaking to Saul himself, but she was suspicious of these strange guests. If she revealed herself as a witch, she was afraid of the king's punishment. But Saul assured her she wouldn't be punished.

"Whom shall I bring up for you?" she finally asked.

"Bring up Samuel for me."

Then the woman saw Samuel, and through this vision she realized it was Saul who stood before her. "Why have you deceived me? You are Saul."

"Have no fear," Saul replied. "What do you see?"

"I see a god coming up out of the earth."

"What is his appearance?" Saul asked.

"An old man is coming up; and he is wrapped in a robe."

Saul knew it was Samuel who stood in their midst, and he bowed.

Then Saul heard the voice of Samuel speaking to him. "Why have you disturbed me by bringing me up?"

"I am in great distress; for the Philistines are warring against me, and God has turned away from me and answers me no more. . . . I have summoned you to tell me what I shall do."

Samuel replied, "Why then do you ask me, since the Lord has turned from you and become your enemy? The Lord has done to you as he spoke by me; for the Lord has torn the kingdom out of your hand, and given it to your neighbor, David. Because you did not obey the voice of the Lord . . . therefore the Lord has done this thing to you this day. Moreover the Lord will give Israel also with you into the hand of the Philistines; and tomorrow you and your sons shall be with me; the Lord will give the army of Israel also into the hand of the Philistines."

Saul fainted and fell to the ground, terrorized by Samuel's words. When he could speak and listen again, the witch told him she would prepare a meal for him. His servants urged him to eat it. After he had eaten, his strength returned, and he journeyed back to his army.

The next day, the trumpets sounded for battle. The Philistines had the upper hand from the start. Thousands of Israelites were slain, and the rest fled the battlefield. Jonathan and his brothers were killed, and Saul was wounded by arrows.

The king begged his armor-bearer to put him to death so the enemy soldiers would not capture and torture him. But the servant was too afraid and refused. In despair, Saul took his own sword and fell on it. When the armor-bearer saw that Saul was dead, he too fell on his sword.

When the battle was over, the Philistines found the dead bodies of Saul and his sons lying on Mount Gilboa. They cut off Saul's head and stripped him of his armor, and they sent word to all the people that Saul had been slain. They put the armor of the king in the temple of their goddess and hung his body and the bodies of his sons on the walls of the city of Bethshan.

The Israelites who lived at Jabesh-gilead heard what the Philistines had done to Saul. So they chose a band of brave men, who came by night and took the body of Saul and the bodies of his sons and buried them in the woods near Jabesh. Then they fasted in mourning for seven days.

When David heard of Saul's death, he mourned and wept and fasted until evening, for Saul and for Jonathan and for the people of the Lord who had fallen in battle.

Saul's story, which came to such a tragic end, shows how greatness can become corrupted. His downfall began with a distrust and impatience toward God, and it continued with his jealousy of David. Even great leaders can sin because of their fallen human nature.

Even so, through the story of Saul, we meet David, the young boy who was so brave that he stood up to a monstrous man such as Goliath. This was the beginning of David's story, and from there, he went on to other great conquests in battle. We also saw the compassionate side of this great figure as he spared the life of Saul, then mourned when Saul finally died in battle, even though Saul had tried to kill him several times.

Next, we will journey through the reign of David, one of the most important figures in the Old Testament, who was the great royal ancestor of the Savior.

CHAPTER 13

David's Reign

David Accepted as King

Together with his band of faithful soldiers and companions, David went to Hebron, where he was accepted as
the king of the tribe of Judah. He ruled over the tribe of
Judah for seven and a half years before the rest of the nation would accept him as their king. This delay took place
because Saul had a son who was still alive, and Abner,
Saul's general, tried to make him king.

Civil war ensued, and battle after battle was fought.
But finally, Saul's son was slain. The hearts of the people then turned to David, and delegates from the twelve
tribes were sent to him, anointing him king of the whole
nation at Hebron.

David decided to make Jerusalem the capital of the
nation. It was a city built on a hill called Mount Zion,
and the Israelites would have to take it from the Canaanites. Wanting to mock and humiliate David and

his approaching army, the Canaanites placed the lame and the blind among them along the walls of Jerusalem. They shouted taunts at David and his men, laughing and claiming that even these feeble men would keep David from entering the gates.

David offered the command of his army to the first man who scaled the walls of Jerusalem. The reward went to a man named Joab, who would go on to become David's general. Great numbers of David's soldiers followed Joab. They set fire to the city to frighten the people and opened the gates to the rest of the soldiers. Once David took Jerusalem and made it his capital, Jerusalem became known as the City of David.

Tyre was the leading city of the Phoenicians, and Hiram was its king. He saw how the power of the young King David was growing, so he gave up his alliance with the Philistines in favor of the king of the Israelites. He sent him some of the wonderful cedar wood from the Lebanon Mountains, with carpenters and masons to build a palace for him.

This act of Hiram angered the Philistines. They determined to conquer David before he became too powerful. They attacked him twice, coming up the valleys between the hills of Judah, and both times, guided by God, David drove them back.

The people of Israel's tribes were able to maintain unity because of their shared religion. Samuel had told them that as long as they sacrificed to the Lord before the Tabernacle, they would not need a king to keep them together.

In order to attach the people to himself and to his capital city, David decided to bring the Ark of the Covenant to Mount Zion. After its return from the Philistines many years before, the Ark had been left at the house of Abinadab, but now it would be moved.

Guarded by thirty thousand men, the Ark was placed on a new cart drawn by oxen and driven by Abinadab's two sons, Uzzah and Ahio. David and the people formed a procession, walking before the Ark, singing and playing musical instruments.

The procession had gone a great distance when suddenly one of the oxen stumbled. The Ark wavered on top of the cart, threatening to fall to the ground. Uzzah put his hand on the Ark to steady it, but he died immediately, for no one was allowed to touch the Ark except for the priests. Seeing this, David was afraid to proceed any farther with the Ark, so he left it at the house of a Levite.

God blessed the Levite in whose house the Ark rested. So after three months David decided to bring the Ark to his capital city of Jerusalem. He brought with him seven choirs of singers and many calves for the sacrifice. Laying aside his royal robe, he danced before the Ark and played on his harp. The Levites carried the Ark all the way to Jerusalem and placed it in the Tabernacle that David had built for it.

David extended his empire by overcoming the enemies that surrounded the Chosen People on all sides. Three times he defeated the Philistines, and he fought successfully against the other nations, forcing them all to pay tribute to him.

David's Son Revolts

David had a son named Absalom who was ambitious and jealous of his father's position. He determined to become king in his father's place. In preparation, he surrounded himself with a bodyguard of fifty men, giving them horses and chariots.

Absalom had a devious plan to gain a loyal following. When unhappy people came to Jerusalem to plead their cases before the king and obtain his judgment, Absalom would remain nearby and wait for the verdict his father issued. If David ruled against any of the people, Absalom would take them aside and tell them that, if he were king, he would have sided with them. In this way the seeds of his revolt were planted.

Then one day, Absalom obtained his father's permission to go to Hebron, a city several miles south of Jerusalem, where he had been born. This was the place where David had first been proclaimed king.

Absalom said he wanted to go to Hebron so he could fulfill a vow he had made to offer a sacrifice in that city. But his real purpose was to have himself made king there. He expected an army to join him in the south. Then he would return to capture Jerusalem, forcing his father to surrender.

When David heard that Absalom had risen up against him, he fled from Jerusalem, because he wanted to spare the people the misery of an attack. He commanded two priests to remain in Jerusalem with the Ark, and he instructed them to keep him informed of Absalom's intentions.

Absalom and his army entered the city of Jerusalem and took possession of David's palace. He then made every effort to win the people over, hoping they would accept him as their king. When he concluded that he had won their trust, he set out in pursuit of his father.

One of David's followers, a man named Hushai, had remained in Jerusalem to keep the true king informed of all that was going on in the capital. Hushai sent messengers to David, urging him to leave his camp beside the Jordan, where he was hiding. The king obeyed these instructions and fled to the land of Gilead. He was received with open arms by the people there.

Absalom pursued his father to the land of Gilead, and David prepared to meet the attack of his son. He divided his army into three companies, intending to lead one of them himself. But the people of the city persuaded him to remain behind with them where he would be safe.

David's army met the men of Absalom in a wooded valley, where a fierce battle was fought. Absalom's army was defeated, and he was forced to flee. While riding away on a mule, Absalom's long hair was caught in the branch of a tree. He was jerked from the mule's back and left hanging in the air.

Joab, the captain of David's army, found him there and thrust three lances into his heart. Then he took him down and buried him in a pit, piling stones on his grave.

It was Hushai who brought the news of Absalom's death to David. When the king heard that his son was dead, he mourned bitterly and cried out, "O my son Absalom, O Absalom, my son, my son!"

The tribe of Judah determined to restore David to his kingdom, so they sent a great escort to meet the king. When David had crossed the river Jordan at Gilgal, a clash broke out. The other tribes were angry with the tribe of Judah because they hadn't been consulted about bringing David back to the kingdom. But after a brief period of fighting, David put down the revolt.

In the story about David's son, we again see the king's compassionate side. His own son sought to remove him from the throne and have him killed. But after Absalom's death, David still mourned for the young man. In addition, we see that David fled Jerusalem in order to spare the people from a fierce battle.

Clearly, David was a compassionate and talented leader, successful in matters both of state and of war. But we will soon see that even David, in all his greatness, was not free from sin.

David's Sin

It was not much later that David took interest in a woman named Bathsheba. But she was the wife of one of his soldiers, a man named Uriah. David yearned for her so badly that he would stop at nothing to make her his own.

So David committed a grave sin. He gave orders for Uriah to be placed in the front line of battle. Then he commanded Uriah's fellow soldiers to fall back and leave him there alone to be killed. His devious plan worked: Uriah was killed, leaving Bathsheba free to marry David.

Seeing the evil that had infected David's heart, God sent Nathan, the prophet, to talk to him. Nathan approached David and told him a story.

"There were two men in a certain city," Nathan began, "the one rich and the other poor. The rich man had very many flocks and herds; but the poor man had nothing but one little ewe lamb, which he had bought. And he brought it up, and it grew up with him and with his children; it used to eat of his morsel, and drink from his cup, and lie in his bosom, and it was like a daughter to him.

"Now there came a traveler to the rich man, and he was unwilling to take one of his own flock or herd to prepare for the wayfarer who had come to him, but he took the poor man's lamb, and prepared it for the man who had come to him."

When David heard this, he was angry and said to Nathan, "As the Lord lives, the man who has done this deserves to die; and he shall restore the lamb fourfold, because he did this thing, and because he had no pity."

David didn't realize that this story was a fable that symbolized his own actions. David himself was the rich man who had come and stolen the poor man's lamb.

Nathan replied, "You are the man. . . . You have struck down Uriah the Hittite with the sword, and have taken his wife to be your wife, and have slain him with the sword of the Ammonites. Now therefore the sword shall never depart from your house."

In that moment, David realized the evil of his actions. "I have sinned against the Lord!" he exclaimed.

When Nathan saw that David was sorry for his sins and asked God for forgiveness, he said to him, "The Lord . . . has put away your sin; you shall not die. Nevertheless, because by this deed you have utterly scorned the Lord, the child that is born to you shall die."

With those stinging words, Nathan left David.

Not long after, a son was born to David and Bathsheba. The child fell sick, and his life was in danger. David prayed and fasted, but on the seventh day the baby died.

A second son was then born to David and Bathsheba, called Solomon. He was destined to succeed his father on the throne and to rule over the chosen people of God.

David's Legacy

What did David accomplish in his long reign as king over Israel?

At the beginning of his reign, David had dreamed of building a great Temple to God. But the prophet Nathan told him that God had willed for Solomon his son, not him, to build the Temple.

Though he was not allowed to build it, David gathered materials that would be used in its construction. He stored up great amounts of copper, iron, timber, stone, and vast treasures of gold and silver. He also provided the workmen who were to build the Temple.

David called together all the princes of the tribes and the leaders of the army. In their presence, he told Solomon how the Temple should be built. He even gave an exact plan for the furnishings of the house of God.

In support of David, the princes and the leaders of the tribes donated large amounts of gold and silver. The next day David offered sacrifices of one thousand young bulls, one thousand rams, and one thousand lambs to show his appreciation to the princes. It was then that Solomon was publicly anointed during a great ceremony.

It was David who united the Israelites into one great nation, building up a powerful state in the process. He was able to do this because the neighboring nations were small and generally at war with one another, but especially because the Lord was on his side.

Even so, one enemy, the Philistines, were a serious threat to David and his people. They used chariots, horses, and armor in battle, and they always were able to recruit large armies. They also used Canaanite soldiers, men of large stature they had conquered before, when they fought the Israelites.

A change in the way of fighting had begun during Saul's reign. Up to that time, the Israelites depended on the sword and shield for close contact. This style of combat was their preferred way to engage the enemy, but they had to use the sling for distant fighting.

During Saul's time, however, the Israelites began to use the iron-pointed spear, which they threw at their enemy, and the bow and arrow for shooting across long, open distances. Thick armor was also adopted by the Israelites during this time.

David had a strong army to call on. Every man over twenty years old could be enrolled as a soldier.

Before the time of Saul, the heads of the tribes had led a citizen's army in defense of the nation. The army was divided into groups of various sizes, with a commanding officer over each group. Saul had created a standing army, but all citizens had to answer his call when they were needed.

David had added to Saul's troops a company of bodyguards composed of skilled warriors who had been loyal to him while he was in exile. David also had a council of thirty-three wise and brave men who would assist him in battle strategy.

What David didn't have were chariots and cavalry. But his enemies had both. So David crafted a plan to draw the enemy into hilly fields. There the chariots couldn't be used, and the horsemen couldn't attack as a body. The battlefield was then even.

Another battle scheme David used was to focus on putting down the bravest men of the opposing army. The rest, seeing these best men defeated, retreated in terror. Sometimes he sought to kill the leader on whom the soldiers depended. After the death of their leader, the rest of the army usually fled. That was in fact what had happened in his first military battle, when he killed Goliath.

We see, then, why David was able to defeat his enemies, including the mighty Philistines. He had a large standing army with strong and brave commanders who had acquired great fighting skills during their days of exile. They had learned especially how to navigate the mountains, valleys, and rivers, using this skill to their advantage and making sure the terrain could help them win battles.

The heads of the tribes had much authority of their own, but they accepted David's rule. Six thousand Levites were placed throughout the country to represent David as civil officers and judges. The officers gave their orders to the heads of the tribes in David's name, and the heads of the tribes put them into execution. The judges had duties much like those of judges of today.

David built storehouses for grain at convenient places throughout the country. These storehouses were looked after by officers. Vineyards, wine cellars, oil cellars, and the valleys where sheep grazed were cared for by an officer of the king. Plowing and planting were directed by skilled farmers, and orchards were cultivated under expert direction.

In his court David had a civil council, a chief secretary, a chief historian, and a chief tax collector. Two high priests were in charge of the religious ceremonies, while David divided the Levites into groups. Some cared for the Ark, others guarded the treasures collected for the Temple, and still others formed a choir to chant the sacred music.

David was a lover of poetry and music. He wrote beautiful poetry of his own and was an excellent musician. As we have seen, even as a boy he had played the harp for Saul. He composed religious hymns for feast days, known today as Psalms. Many of these are prophetic, foretelling the sufferings and triumph of the Savior to come.

David also trained a group of singers and players for the religious ceremonies of the people. They used many instruments, including the harp, pipe, horn, trumpet, tambourine, cymbal, and triangle.

David wrote one of his most beautiful psalms when Saul was persecuting him. He was thinking of the days when he had been a shepherd boy and had made an act of faith in God, who would take care of him, just as a shepherd cares for his sheep. This psalm provides a fitting end to the story of David:

The Lord is my shepherd, I shall not want;
He makes me lie down in green pastures.
He leads me beside still waters;
He restores my soul.
He leads me in paths of righteousness
for His name's sake.
Even though I walk through the valley of the
    shadow of death,
I fear no evil;
for You are with me;
Your rod and Your staff,
they comfort me.
You prepare a table before me
in the presence of my enemies;

You anoint my head with oil,
my cup overflows.
Surely goodness and mercy shall follow me
all the days of my life;
and I shall dwell in the house of the Lord forever.

Despite the sins David committed during his reign, he was a great king and prophet, and he reigned for forty years, until he died. He formed a strong army and a good government, and he established a capital for the nation. He was deeply religious and was passionate in restoring to its original grandeur the worship of the true God.

David showed sincere repentance for his sins, and so he is a model for sinners seeking forgiveness. His kingdom pointed toward the kingdom of heaven, which the Savior, the greatest of his descendants, would one day establish on earth. At his death, that kingdom would be entrusted to his son, the wise King Solomon.

CHAPTER 14

The Israelites Under King Solomon

Solomon's Wisdom

Solomon, the son of David and Bathsheba, was not yet twenty years old when he became king. Feeling his inexperience, he went to Gibeon, where the Tabernacle stood, to offer a sacrifice to God and ask for His blessing. Solomon sought God's guidance for his coming reign. He offered one thousand animals to God at this time.

That night, God spoke to Solomon and asked him to name the gifts that he desired. Solomon asked only one thing: *wisdom* to govern his people well. God was pleased because Solomon had asked for wisdom rather than for wealth or power.

Answering the young king's prayer, God made him the wisest of all the rulers of his time. Besides wisdom, God gave Solomon the wealth, glory, and power that he hadn't sought. The Lord also promised him a long life if he would obey His law.

One day, two women came to Solomon to have him settle a dispute that had arisen between them. Both of them had infants of about the same age. In the middle of the night, the baby that belonged to one of them died. The mother of the dead child took away the living child and left the other in its place. The next morning, when the other woman discovered what had been done, she came to the king and demanded that her child be given back to her.

Both women stood before the king, and each claimed that the child was her own. But Solomon knew how to have them reveal the truth. He asked for a sword, then ordered an attendant to cut the child in half and give half of it to each woman.

When the true mother heard this command, she cried out, "Oh, my lord, give her the living child, and by no means slay it."

But the other woman said, "It shall be neither mine nor yours; divide it."

Solomon knew at once who had told the truth. The true mother was willing to give up her child rather than see it die. But the other woman was content to see both children dead.

So Solomon commanded: "Give the living child to the first woman, and by no means slay it; she is its mother." Then the child was restored to the woman who had pleaded for its life.

Many of the wise things that Solomon said are found in the Book of Proverbs. Soon, his wisdom was known throughout the world, and neighboring nations spoke of him with great admiration.

Eventually, his reputation spread to a queen who ruled over a small city-state called Sheba. She was not convinced that everything she had heard about Solomon was true. So she decided to go to Jerusalem to see for herself.

The queen set out from Sheba, her royal city, and came

to Jerusalem with presents of gold and precious stones. Solomon received her kindly and permitted her to ask him all sorts of difficult questions as she tested his wisdom. But nothing she asked was able to baffle Solomon.

When she left to go home, the queen said to him, "The report was true which I heard in my own land of your affairs and of your wisdom, but I did not believe the reports until I came and my own eyes had seen it; and behold, the half was not told me; your wisdom and prosperity surpass the report which I heard. . . . Blessed be the Lord your God, who has delighted in you and set you on the throne of Israel!"

Solomon Builds the Temple

No sooner had Solomon ascended the throne than he began to prepare for the building of the Temple. He made an agreement with King Hiram to furnish fir and cedar trees from the Lebanon Mountains. Hiram had the wood brought to the sea and floated down, where it was taken by land to Jerusalem.

For this labor and material, Solomon paid Hiram annually with one hundred and forty gallons of olive oil and twenty-five hundred bushels of wheat. Solomon sent his own men to the Lebanon Mountains to help the servants of King Hiram. They worked in shifts: one month of labor, followed by two months of rest. It took many men to find and transport the required materials.

The construction of the Temple was begun in the fourth year of Solomon's reign and took more than seven years to complete. During its erection there was no noise of a hammer, for every beam and stone was carefully cut and fitted beforehand. In general, the Temple followed the design of the Tabernacle and faced the east, but it was double the size. It was situated on an elevation to the east of the city.

The outside wall enclosed the *Court of the Gentiles*. (The Gentiles are people who aren't Jewish.) On a higher level,

within and separated by another wall, was the *Court of the Israelites.* Within this and still higher was the *Court of the Priests,* which surrounded the main Temple area. This last court contained the altar of holocausts and the *bronze basin.* This basin was also known as the *bronze sea,* a huge bowl of bronze resting on twelve bronze oxen, three facing each point of the compass. It held about ten thousand gallons of water so the priests could wash their bodies before a sacrifice. There were also ten smaller ones that were movable.

At the east end of the structure was the *Porch,* or vestibule, of the Temple. It was framed by enormous pillars on either side.

Beyond the Porch and separated from it by folding doors was *the Holy Place,* sixty feet long, thirty feet wide and forty-five feet high. The entire room was lined with richly carved cedar wood covered with gold. Here stood the golden altar of incense, the golden table containing the loaves of show-bread, and the golden seven-branched candlesticks.

At the western end was the *Holy of Holies,* much like the Holy of Holies in the Tabernacle. Lined in gold, it was the shape of a thirty-foot cube. Before the entrance to this room hung a richly woven veil that covered the interior. This room contained nothing but the Ark of the Covenant, with its golden images of adoring cherubim.

In autumn of the year in which the Temple was finished, on the Feast of Tabernacles, the priests and the Levites brought the Ark of the Covenant to the Holy of Holies in the Temple. The Levites brought the Tabernacle and its furnishings from Gibeon.

At the dedication of the Temple, twenty-two thousand oxen and one hundred and twenty thousand sheep were offered in adoration to God. Solomon gave thanks and, after his prayer, fire came down from heaven to consume the sacrifices.

People from every part of Solomon's kingdom came to the dedication of the Temple, staying with him and feasting for fourteen days. At this time God again spoke to Solomon. He promised to protect the king and his people as long as they walked as He had instructed them.

In building the Temple, the Israelites once again obeyed the command of the Law to worship God in one place. The Temple was intended to forge a bond of union among the tribes. But other factors divided them from one another and brought about lasting strife.

Prosperity Leads to Division and Unrest
When the Temple was about half finished, Solomon began to build his palace, which consisted of four parts. There was a large assembly hall packed full of gold furniture, called the *House of the Forest of Lebanon.* The *Hall of the Throne* contained Solomon's ivory throne covered with gold, which he built himself. He pronounced judgments for the people there.

The third part of his palace was the house in which he dined and slept, while the fourth unit was the house for his Egyptian wife. In the front of the palace was a porch, used as a reception hall, and in the back stood a court filled with fountains and gardens.

Solomon's neighbors didn't interfere in his affairs until near the end of his life. The empire built up by David extended from the Euphrates to Egypt, and it remained intact during the forty years of Solomon's reign. It was this reign of peace that made Solomon's days the golden age of the kingdom of Israel.

Solomon protected his kingdom and his traders. He fortified the Temple and palace and built a city to protect his caravans coming in from the East. He also erected fortresses along the northern frontier and in the plains.

The king carried on trade with neighboring countries. His contact with King Hiram taught him the value of commerce. His caravan routes led to the lands of the Hittites, the Syrians, and the Babylonians, and Egypt sent him horses and chariots. King Hiram built ships for him, and he paid sailors to guide them. He sent these ships to India for ivory and gold, and to Spain for gold and silver.

Solomon received great wealth from his caravans and ships, as well as from rents and taxes. The neighboring states presented him with expensive gifts each year, and his income in gold was enormous. Besides all this, he received cattle and provisions from his own kingdom.

The money for the building of the Temple had been saved by David. But Solomon's expenses were heavy. To meet these expenses, the people were taxed on every article they bought, and they were forced to supply Solomon with meat and grain. It didn't take long for the people to become dissatisfied with these heavy taxes.

Fearing that the Temple would not be sufficient to

keep the people attached to the king in Jerusalem, Solomon divided the country into twelve provinces instead of the traditional tribal divisions. He thought this new arrangement would destroy the jealousies that had existed among the tribes and prevent future civil wars.

But Solomon forgot the one important means for keeping the people united with him. He neglected to worship the true God. His heavy taxes caused the people to hate him and prepared them to follow the first strong leader who would rise up against him.

Had Solomon remained true to God, he could have pointed to the Temple and rallied the people around him again. But he didn't remain true to God. As he grew older, he became too fond of pleasure, and his great wisdom left him. To please his wives from foreign countries, he built temples to their false gods. This act destroyed the religious unity of the Israelites, without which there could be no national unity.

Taxation and idolatry, then, were the two major factors that led to the breakup of Jewish unity, the unity that King David had fervently desired.

A Rebel Leader

The people were now ready for a rebellion, and a man named Jeroboam was preparing himself to be the leader of that rebellion. He was a brave and talented man whom Solomon had put in charge of the fortifications of Jerusalem. Later the king also gave him the office of collecting the tribute from several different tribes.

One day when Jeroboam was going out of the city of Jerusalem, he met the prophet Ahijah, who was dressed in a new cloak. Ahijah walked along with him until they came into the open country.

Then, taking off his new cloak, Ahijah tore it into twelve pieces and said to Jeroboam, "Take for yourself ten pieces; for thus says the Lord, the God of Israel, 'Behold, I am about to tear the kingdom from the hand of Solomon, and will give you ten tribes . . . because he has forsaken me, and worshiped Ashtoreth the goddess of the Sidonians, Chemosh the god of Moab, and Milcom the god of the Ammonites, and has not walked in My ways, doing what is right in My sight and keeping My statues and My ordinances, as David his father did . . .

"But I will take the kingdom out of his son's hand, and will give it to you, ten tribes. Yet to his son I will give one tribe, that David My servant may always have a lamp before Me in Jerusalem, the city where I have chosen to put My name. And I will take you, and you shall reign over all that your soul desires, and you shall be king over Israel."

Jeroboam was filled with confidence after hearing these words from the prophet. Solomon's practice of taxing the people gave Jeroboam plenty of opportunities to turn the people against their king. He encouraged their discontent and tried to make himself popular with them.

When Solomon discovered that Jeroboam was turning the people against him, he tried to have him killed. But Jeroboam escaped and fled into Egypt. It was not long, however, before Solomon died, and after a reign of forty years, he was buried in Jerusalem.

Can you see a pattern throughout the history of the Old Testament—a pattern that still takes place today? How many times do we see a time of happiness and prosperity followed by a period of decline? It's easy to forget about God and how much we need Him when things are going well.

Solomon is one more example of a man who rose to greatness, but was tempted by earthly treasures at the peak of his success and turned his back on God. Because of his sins, the golden age of his reign was lost, and more chaos ensued for the Israelites.

CHAPTER 15

Jeroboam and Rehoboam

Rehoboam's Reign

After the death of Solomon, his son, Rehoboam, went to Shechem, where he hoped to be anointed king. He was met by representatives of the people who told him that before they would recognize him as their king, they had certain demands to make. They asked that the taxes his father had imposed on them be reduced.

Rehoboam requested three days to consider their request, and called together his father's counselors to ask them what he should do. They advised him to lighten the burden of the people and reduce the taxes. Next, he called together a number of young men, friends and companions from his youth. They advised him to do the opposite, to continue to demand the heavy taxes, because he would need the money if he were to continue to live in splendor as his father had lived.

Rehoboam listened to his young friends instead of his

father's older counselors. He sent for the representatives of the people and said to them, "My father made your yoke heavy, but I will add to your yoke; my father chastised you with whips, but I will chastise you with scorpions."

When the people heard that Rehoboam planned to increase their burden rather than reduce it, they rose up in revolt. He sent Adoram, an overseer of the forced laborers, to calm them. But the people stoned him to death.

Rehoboam, realizing that his life was in danger, fled to Jerusalem in his chariot. There, he intended to raise an army and force the rebels to obey him. But the voice of God came to the prophet Shemaiah, telling Rehoboam that he was not to attack. So Rehoboam, fearing the Lord, obeyed the warning of the prophet.

The tribes of Judah and Benjamin remained loyal to Rehoboam. But the other ten tribes chose as their king Jeroboam, the leader of the rebellion against Solomon. The Levites aligned themselves with Rehoboam when they saw that Jeroboam was leading his people into idolatry, worshipping false gods.

Rehoboam fortified the towns of Judah and Benjamin, which were all that was left to him of the great kingdom of his father. From then on, it was known as the Kingdom of Judah, or the Southern Kingdom, while the kingdom Jeroboam established was known as the Kingdom of Israel, or the Northern Kingdom.

Jeroboam the Idolater

Jeroboam would not allow the people of his ten tribes to worship in the Temple at Jerusalem. He thought it was necessary to keep them from the Temple in order to keep them loyal to himself rather than to God. To make the division of the tribes lasting, he founded a new state religion.

Jeroboam built two temples. One was in the northern part of his kingdom, in the city of Dan, and the other was in the south, in the city of Bethel. He set up a golden calf in each of them, much like the golden calf that the Israelites had worshiped in the wilderness many years before.

"You have gone up to Jerusalem long enough," the king told the people. "Behold your gods, O Israel, who brought you up out of the land of Egypt!"

To recruit priests for this idolatrous worship, Jeroboam allowed any man to fulfill the role if he could provide a young bull and seven rams for sacrifice. In addition, the king allowed altars to be built to the false gods throughout his kingdom.

Jeroboam made Shechem his capital, a city closely connected with the founders of the Israelite nation. There, Abraham had settled when he first came from Ur into the Promised Land, and Jacob too had lived there for some time. Both of them had built altars in Shechem, and Jacob had dug a well nearby. It was also in the fields of Shechem that Joseph looked for his brothers, and there his bones were buried when the Israelites returned from Egypt.

All these connections to the past made Shechem an ideal place for Jeroboam to erect his capital. In this way, he was appealing to the people's patriotism.

Shortly after the institution of the state religion, Jeroboam was worshiping the golden calf at Bethel when a prophet from the kingdom of Judah prophesied to him. The prophet foretold that a future king, Josiah, would burn the false priests of Jeroboam on an altar, and that a sign would occur to let the people know this prophecy had been fulfilled. The prophet also said that the altar of worship was about to be broken, and the ashes would be scattered about on the ground.

When he heard these threatening words, Jeroboam pointed at the prophet and called for his men to take him captive. Suddenly, the hand with which he was pointing became withered, the altar was broken in two, and the ashes were scattered on the ground.

Jeroboam was terrified and asked the prophet to pray on his behalf. The prophet did so, and Jeroboam's hand was healed.

Later, Jeroboam's son became very ill. Jeroboam sent his wife to see the prophet Ahijah in Shiloh, to inquire about their son's health. But he told her to disguise herself so the prophet wouldn't know she was the queen.

When she knocked at his door, God told the prophet who she was, that she was the queen and the wife of Jeroboam, and that she had come to ask about her sick son. So the prophet saw right past her disguise and addressed her as the wife of Jeroboam.

He gave her a message to deliver to her husband.

"Thus says the Lord, the God of Israel: 'I exalted you from among the people, and made you leader over my people Israel, and tore the kingdom away from the house of David and gave it to you; and yet you have not been like my servant David, who kept my commandments, and followed me with all his heart, doing only that which was right in my eyes, but you have done evil above all that were before you and have gone and made for yourself other gods, and molten images, provoking me to anger, and have cast me behind your back; therefore behold, I will bring evil on the house of Jeroboam.'"

The prophet reported that Jeroboam would be rooted out of the land, and his son would die. The Kingdom of Israel would be overthrown by the Assyrians, who would lead the people into captivity. The queen left frightened and returned to her city to find that her son had died, just as Ahijah had prophesied.

Rehoboam's Descendants and Their Kingdom

Although Rehoboam's kingdom consisted of only two tribes, it was strong, and the tribe of Judah had a spirit of unity. Their leaders were from the family of David and Solomon, and they shared the reputation of those two great kings. The Temple was in their kingdom, and the people sacrificed on one altar there alone, according to the Law.

For three years Rehoboam remained a just and God-fearing ruler. But eventually he followed evil advice and built altars to pagan gods in various parts of the kingdom. Rehoboam set an example of idolatry, just as Jeroboam had done, and the people followed it.

Because of this idolatry, God permitted the Pharaoh of Egypt at that time to invade the Kingdom of Judah. He entered Jerusalem with sixty thousand horsemen, twelve hundred chariots, and a great number of foot soldiers. He stole the treasures of the Temple and the king's palace.

This attack worked nicely into the plan of Jeroboam. He knew that as long as Rehoboam was troubled by the Egyptians, he couldn't turn his attention to the rival Kingdom of Israel.

Meanwhile, the neighboring nations were growing in power. Egypt, Assyria, and Babylonia were all pursuing their own interests. Even the united kingdom of David and Solomon would have needed its greatest strength to preserve its independence against such powerful enemies. But now God's people were split up into helpless divisions, some standing firm with Rehoboam, and others with Jeroboam.

Prosperity had come to an end, because neither king was strong enough to trade with other countries. Meanwhile, civil wars ruined great portions of the country. Great numbers of soldiers on the battlefield meant great numbers of men taken from the trades and agriculture; as soldiers, many of these good men died. Scarcity of food and a high cost of living naturally followed.

Rehoboam died after reigning for seventeen years. He was succeeded by his son, Abijam, who would go on to reign for three years. Abijam fought successfully against Jeroboam and drove him back into his own territory, capturing many cities near the border of his kingdom.

A period of peace for the Southern Kingdom then followed. Asa, the son of Abijam, became king, and he governed the nation wisely. For ten years the people devoted themselves to peaceful pursuits and grew in wealth. During this time Asa destroyed the places where idols were worshiped.

In the Northern Kingdom, however, no such peace and prosperity were to be found. God had to send a mighty prophet to speak to the people there and call them back to His ways.

CHAPTER 16

Elijah the Prophet

Elijah Speaks the Word of God

The Kingdom of Israel was torn by plots and dissensions. The people bickered and fought, and they were divided into two factions. After the death of Jeroboam, Omri, the general of the army, was made king by his own troops, and he ruled one part of Israel. But the other part was ruled by a man named Tibni. Finally, Omri's forces defeated Tibni's forces, and Tibni was killed in battle. That left Omri as the only king.

Because of this civil war, Tirzah, the capital of Israel's kingdom, was left in ruins. So Omri bought a hill northwest of Shechem and made it the new capital of his kingdom. He called it Samaria.

When Omri died, his son, Ahab, became king. He was a wicked man who married a cruel and idolatrous woman named Jezebel. To please Jezebel, Ahab built in Samaria a temple to the pagan god Baal.

God then sent to the king a man named Elijah, a prophet and a brave and fearless man. The prophet told Ahab that because of his sins of idolatry, the land would suffer a great drought. For three years no rain would fall.

After Elijah had foretold the drought, God directed him to go to the brook called Cherith.

"You shall drink from the brook," God told him, "and I have commanded the ravens to feed you there."

So the prophet went there, and each morning and evening a raven would bring him bread and meat to eat. He drank from the brook as the Lord had commanded.

But soon the brook dried up, for just as Elijah himself had predicted, a drought had begun to plague the land. God then directed him to go to Zarephath, a city near Sidon, where a widow would feed him. When Elijah came to the gate of the city, he saw the widow gathering sticks.

He called to her and said, "Bring me a little water in a vessel, that I may drink." As she went to retrieve the water, he added, "Bring me a morsel of bread in your hand."

But the woman told Elijah that she had no food to spare. She barely had enough to feed her son and herself. She told him that soon they would die of starvation.

Elijah told the woman not to be afraid. She should still share whatever food she had with him, because the Lord would maintain their food supply until the drought was over. She went and did as Elijah had said, and from that day forward until the end of the famine, her food supply remained steady.

One day, however, the son of the widow became ill and died. She shouted at Elijah: "What have you against me, O man of God?"

Elijah was grateful to the woman who had fed him and was grieved by her son's death. He took the boy away from her and begged God to bring him back to life. The

Lord heard Elijah's prayer, and He raised the boy from the dead.

Elijah returned and gave the son to his mother, saying, "See, your son lives."

The woman replied, "Now I know that you are a man of God, and that the word of the Lord in your mouth is true."

Elijah's Challenge to the Pagans
Because of the drought, Ahab had many of the prophets of the true God killed. He wanted to kill Elijah, too,

but he searched for him in vain throughout the kingdom. He sent messengers to the neighboring nations to seek the prophet, but they couldn't find him, either.

In the third year of the drought, God said to Elijah, "Go, show yourself to Ahab; and I will send rain upon the earth."

So Elijah went to Samaria, where the drought was especially bad. But Ahab and the governor of his household, Obadiah, had gone out across the land in search of food for the horses and mules, to save them from death. Ahab went one way and Obadiah another.

On the way, Obadiah met Elijah and recognized him. Obadiah was a good man. He had hidden one hundred prophets from danger when Ahab was seeking their lives. He provided them with bread and water to keep them alive. Obadiah loved and honored the true God, so he respected Elijah.

He bowed low and asked, "Is it you, my lord Elijah?"

"It is I," Elijah answered, "Go, tell your lord, 'Elijah is here.'"

Obadiah hesitated to follow Elijah's instructions. He was afraid that once he told the king where to find the prophet, God would hide the prophet again. Then, when Ahab couldn't find him, Obadiah would be executed for deceiving him. But Elijah assured Obadiah that he would remain to meet the king.

So Obadiah took the message to Ahab, and Ahab came to meet Elijah.

When the two of them met, Elijah told Ahab to gather together at Mount Carmel the people of Israel, including the priests of the false god Baal. Ahab did so, and when the people assembled, Elijah spoke to them, hoping to lead them back to the one true God.

"How long will you go limping with two different opinions?" he asked. "If the Lord is God, follow him; but if Baal, then follow him. . . . I, even I only, am left a prophet of the Lord; but Baal's prophets are four hundred and fifty men.

"Let two bulls be given to us; and let them choose one bull for themselves, and cut it in pieces and lay it on the wood, but put no fire to it; and I will prepare the other bull and lay it on the wood, and put no fire to it. And you call on the name of your god and I will call on the name of the Lord; and the God who answers by fire, he is God."

The people were willing to make this test of their god, to see which bull would be consumed by fire: the bull of Baal or the bull of the true God. So the prophets of Baal called on the name of Baal from morning till noon, begging for fire, even leaping over the altar they had made. But it was all in vain; there was no answer.

At noon, with the sun high in the sky, Elijah mocked them.

"Cry aloud," he said, "for he is a god; either he is musing, or he has gone aside, or he is on a journey, or perhaps he is asleep and must be awakened."

They cried out even louder, egged on by his taunts, and cut themselves with their knives till they were covered with blood. But no answer came to their prayers.

Then Elijah said to the people, "Come near to me." So the people approached him.

He built an altar to the Lord with twelve stones, one for each of the twelve tribes of Israel. Then he made a trench for water. He placed his bull on the wood and he had twelve buckets of water poured over the bull. The water ran around the altar and filled the trench.

When it was time to offer the sacrifice, Elijah came near to the altar and said, "O Lord, God of Abraham, Isaac, and Israel, let it be known this day that You are God in Israel, and that I am Your servant, and that I have done all these things at Your word. Answer me, O Lord, answer me, that this people may know that You, O Lord, are God, and that You have turned their hearts back."

At that moment, the fire of the Lord fell and consumed the offering. The fire was so great that it even dried up the water in the trench! When all the people saw this, they fell on their faces and cried: "The Lord, He is God; the Lord, He is God."

Elijah commanded the people to take the prophets of Baal to the brook Kishon, which flowed at the foot of Mount Carmel. There, at God's command, Elijah put them all to death.

Elijah has been called the greatest prophet of the Old Testament. He appeared at a critical time in the history of the Israelites, working miracles to get their attention, calling them back to God, and showing the futility of worshipping false gods. But his triumph over the priests of Baal put him in great danger, so he had to flee once again. While he was in exile, God told him about his final mission, and the man who would take his place as a prophet of the Lord.

Elijah Finds Elisha, His Disciple

Jezebel, Ahab's wicked wife, was furious when she heard what Elijah had done to the priests and prophets of Baal. She sent threats to Elijah, warning that the same death awaited him. In fear, Elijah fled the country.

After traveling for quite some time, he was exhausted. So he sat down in the desert a short distance from the city of Beersheba. He was so tired, hungry, and afraid that he begged God to kill him.

"It is enough; now, O Lord, take away my life; for I am no better than my fathers."

He then fell asleep under a tree. Soon an angel came to him and brought him food, saying, "Arise and eat."

Elijah rose up and found a cake baked on hot stones and a jar of water for him. He ate and drank, then went back to sleep. Again a second time the angel came to him and said, "Arise and eat, else the journey will be too great for you."

He rose up again and ate, and he gained such strength from the food that he walked for forty days and forty nights to Horeb, the mountain of God. There he lived in a cave.

One day the Lord appeared to Elijah and told him to go to the wilderness of Damascus. When he arrived there, he was to anoint one man to be king over Syria, and another to be king of Israel. A third man, named Elisha, was to be anointed as prophet in Elijah's place.

As Elijah was returning to the Northern Kingdom, he found Elisha plowing in a field. Elijah came up to him and threw his mantle over his shoulders. Elisha left his oxen and ran after Elijah and said, "Let me kiss my father and my mother, and then I will follow you."

Elisha then followed Elijah and served him, becoming his disciple.

The relations between the Kingdom of Judah and the Kingdom of Israel were now friendly. But Benhadad, the king of Syria, tried to capture Samaria for his own kingdom. A prophet had informed Ahab that God would grant him victory over the Syrian king. So he set out with an army of seven thousand men and drove the enemy back.

During the second year, the same king returned with a powerful army. Ahab went out again to meet him with a small army and again defeated him with ease. But Ahab spared the life of the king and his counselors, making a treaty with him. The prophet told Ahab that because he had spared the life of the king of Syria, who was worthy of death for his blasphemy, he would lose his own life through a violent death.

Ahab and Jezebel Wrong Naboth

Now there was a man named Naboth who owned a vineyard near the palace of Ahab. The king wanted this vineyard and offered Naboth a different vineyard in another location, or the price of it in money. But because the vineyard was an inheritance from his father, Naboth refused to sell it.

This refusal angered Ahab and his wife, Jezebel. Jezebel paid two men to tell lies and spread rumors about Naboth, saying that he had spoken against God and the king. When the people heard this they took Naboth outside the city and stoned him to death.

Hearing that Naboth was dead, Ahab went and took possession of the vineyard. On his way he met the prophet Elijah, who was sent to him by God. The prophet said to Ahab, "In the place where dogs licked up the blood of Naboth shall dogs lick your own blood."

Elijah also foretold that the dogs would eat the flesh of Jezebel because of her wickedness. The Kingdom of Israel would pass from the house of Ahab because he had caused Israel to sin and offend God.

When Ahab heard these words, he was shamed into doing penance. He tore his clothes, put on sackcloth, and fasted. God was pleased with the penance and the humility of Ahab. He said to Elijah, "Because he has humbled himself before me, I will not bring the evil in his days; but in his son's days I will bring the evil upon his house."

Ahab and Jehoshaphat, the king of Judah, would eventually make another campaign against the king of Syria. Four hundred false prophets promised that the campaign would be a victory for Ahab. But Micaiah, the prophet of the true God, foretold a defeat for Ahab and Jehoshaphat. This ominous prophecy got him thrown into the prison, while the two kings went forward with their campaign.

Ahab disguised himself before going into battle, so that the enemy would not know who he was. But in battle he was shot by a stray arrow, and he died. Later, after he was buried, his blood-stained chariot was brought to a nearby vineyard where it could be washed.

There, dogs licked up his blood, just as they had licked up the blood of Naboth in that same spot. Later, his wife, Jezebel, was also killed by the enemy, and before she could be buried, a dog ate her corpse. In both cases, the words of the prophet Elijah were fulfilled.

Elijah Is Taken to Heaven
While Ahab was ruling over the Kingdom of Israel, Jehoshaphat was king of Judah. He was a wise and peace-loving king and remained true to God all the days of his life. Because of his peaceful nature, there was peace in his country, so the people turned their attention to the trades. They cared for the farms and the pastures, leading to bountiful crops and large and healthy herds. Jehoshaphat also appointed judges in all the chief cities.

But the kings of Judah who succeeded Jehoshaphat were weak and sinful, and the kings of Israel who succeeded Ahab were also evil men. They worshiped idols and forced the people to follow their example. War, disease, and death followed as the consequence of the sinful lives of these kings.

During the reign of Jehoshaphat, Elijah and Elisha were leaving Gilgal. On their journey, Elijah instructed Elisha to stay where he was, for Elijah was going to Bethel. But Elisha refused and swore that he would stay by Elijah's side, just as any disciple would do.

So they went to Bethel together. Again, Elijah instructed Elisha to stay, while he went on to Jericho. But again Elisha refused, and so together they went on to Jericho. Still a third time, Elijah told Elisha to stay while he went on to the Jordan. Again, Elisha refused and stayed by Elijah's side.

And so they came to the Jordan, and when they stood beside it, Elijah rolled up his cloak and struck the water. At once, the water was divided, leaving a dry path through it. They both passed over.

When they had crossed the Jordan, Elijah said to Elisha, "Ask what I shall do for you, before I am taken from you."

Elisha had sensed that the time for Elijah to leave him was nearing. He replied, "I pray you, let me inherit a double share of your spirit."

"You have asked a hard thing," Elijah responded. "Yet, if you see me as I am being taken from you, it shall be so for you; but if you do not see me, it shall not be so."

Then, as they were walking along and talking, a fiery chariot pulled by horses came between them, and Elijah went up by a whirlwind into the heavens. Elisha saw him and cried, "My father, my father! The chariots of Israel and its horsemen!"

A moment later, Elisha could no longer see him. He took up the cloak of Elijah that had fallen on him, and with it he divided the waters, just as Elijah had done, so that he could cross back over the Jordan.

Several men who had also witnessed this event begged Elisha to let them search for Elijah, wondering whether the Lord had taken him to a nearby mountain in this fiery chariot. At first Elisha refused, but when they persisted he sent them off. They couldn't find Elijah, but they believed that his spirit now rested on Elisha.

Elisha Works Miracles

After Elijah's departure, Elisha performed several miracles. Through God's power he purified tainted water in the city of Jericho, raised a young boy from the dead, multiplied oil, caused an iron axe head to float, and multiplied a small portion of food to feed one hundred men.

One notable miracle was the healing of Naaman, the general of the Syrian army. He was brave, rich, and honorable, but he had contracted leprosy. His wife's maid, who was an Israelite, casually mentioned one day that if Naaman were able to see the holy man Elisha, he might be cured.

When the king of Syria heard of the wonderful prophet in Israel, he sent Naaman, his general, to Elisha, begging that he be cured. Naaman went with his horses and chariots and stood waiting at the door of Elisha.

The prophet sent a messenger to Naaman, saying, "Go

and wash in the Jordan seven times, and your flesh shall be restored, and you shall be clean."

Naaman was insulted that Elisha had not himself come to the door to see him, but rather had sent a messenger to give instructions about this strange task. "I thought that he would surely come out to me," he said, "and stand, and call on the name of the Lord his God, and wave his hand over the place, and cure the leper." He wondered why he couldn't wash in one of the rivers of his native land instead of a river in Israel.

The general turned to leave, but his servants convinced him that obedience to the prophet's command was a small price to pay for his health. So Naaman swallowed his pride and went down to wash seven times in the Jordan. When he did, his flesh was restored like the flesh of a little child, and he was cleansed from his leprosy.

Naaman returned to Elisha and thanked him, offering him gifts as a sign of gratitude. But Elisha refused the gifts. Naaman left promising never to adore any other god but the God of Israel.

After Naaman left, Elisha's servant, Gehazi, chased after the general secretly. Gehazi wanted to take for himself the gifts that Elisha had refused. Overcome by his greed, he told Naaman that Elisha had changed his mind and wanted the gifts. So Naaman gave them to Gehazi, who took them back to his own house.

When he returned, Elisha asked, "Where have you been, Gehazi?"

"Your servant went nowhere," Gehazi replied.

But Elisha saw through this lie. He promised that the leprosy that had left Naaman's body would plague Gehazi's body. And it was so. Gehazi left from Elisha's presence afflicted with the disease.

The power to work miracles remained with Elisha even after his death. One day, a burial was taking place near the cave where the prophet had been buried long before. Suddenly, a band of raiders appeared, disrupting the ceremony. The body of the dead man was quickly laid in the cave to protect it from the raiders, and it happened to touch Elisha's bones. When it did, the dead man was restored to life.

We should note that some of the miracles Elisha performed are similar to those that Jesus would perform centuries later. Jesus also cured lepers, raised the dead, and multiplied food to feed a large number of people. But Elisha, even though he was a holy man of God, was not the Son of God as Jesus was. Instead, Elisha's miracles were a foreshadowing of the ones Jesus performed, much as Abraham's willingness to sacrifice his son Isaac had been a foreshadowing of God the Father's sacrifice of His Son, Jesus.

Other examples of foreshadowing appear in the Old Testament, pointing toward important events in the New Testament. We'll find one of those examples in another story we'll encounter soon.

CHAPTER 17

The Stories of Job and Jonah

The Origins of Job and His Misfortunes

Job was a holy and wealthy man from the land of Uz. We don't know exactly where Uz was located, but it was probably in Edom, the country that bordered the southern shore of the Dead Sea.

Job lived in a house built of stone with his seven sons and three daughters. He had many servants to wait on him. He owned seven thousand sheep, three thousand camels, five hundred yoke of oxen, and five hundred donkeys.

On a certain day, when the angels came to stand before God, Satan was present among them. The Lord said to Satan, "Have you considered my servant Job, that there is none like him on the earth, a blameless and upright man, who fears God and turns away from evil?"

Satan answered the Lord, "Does Job fear God for naught? Have You not put a hedge about him and his house and all that he has, on every side? You have blessed the work of his hands, and his possessions have increased in the land. But put forth Your hand now, and touch all that he has, and he will curse You to Your face."

Satan was claiming that Job loved God only because he was a blessed man. The Lord then agreed to let Satan test Job, saying, "Behold, all that he has is in your power; only upon himself do not put forth your hand."

So Satan left the presence of the Lord and set his sights squarely on Job.

Great disasters then came upon Job. One day, a servant came to Job to tell him that raiders from nearby lands had rushed into the fields where his oxen were plowing and taken them all away. Then, the raiders had killed all the servants who were working in this field, except this one messenger who had escaped.

While this servant was speaking, another servant came to tell him that in a different location, lightning from heaven had killed all his sheep and the servants who were tending them. Only this one servant had escaped to tell Job about it.

While he was speaking, yet another servant came to say that more hostile men had come and taken Job's camels away. They had killed the servants who were watching over them, except for this one servant who had gotten away.

While he was speaking, still another servant came in and told Job that a violent wind had shaken the house of his eldest son, where his sons and daughters were feasting. The house fell on his children and killed them all. Only this one servant had managed to get out before the house collapsed.

In that brief span, Job had lost his oxen, sheep, camels, dozens of servants, and most importantly, his children.

After all this, Job rose and, as a sign of sorrow, tore his clothes and shaved his head. Then he fell on the ground and worshiped God, saying, "Naked I came from my mother's womb, and naked shall I return; the Lord gave, and the Lord has taken away; blessed be the name of the Lord."

In all this, Job did not sin or blame God.

Meanwhile, Satan returned to stand before God. God said to him, "Have you considered my servant Job, that there is none like him on the earth, a blameless and upright man, who fears God and turns away from evil? He still holds fast his integrity, although you moved Me against him, to destroy him without cause."

Satan answered, "All that a man has he will give for his life. But put forth Your hand now, and touch his bone and his flesh, and he will curse You to Your face."

The Lord said to Satan, "He is in your power; only spare his life."

So Satan went forth with plans to destroy Job's health. He struck him with ulcers that covered him from the sole of his foot to the top of his head. Job was in terrible pain, but he didn't blame God.

Job's wife ridiculed him because he actually blessed God in his suffering. "Do you still hold fast your integrity?" she said. "Curse God, and die."

But Job pointed out that up until now, they had received many blessings from the Lord. So why shouldn't they accept these hardships as well?

Job cried out in sorrow and pain, and his friends came to him. But instead of consoling him, they added new sorrows. They didn't realize that God had allowed Satan to test Job with these hardships. So they rebuked him and told him he was being punished for his sins.

But Job himself knew that this was no punishment for

his sins. He told his friends that even though he suffered greatly, he still trusted in God. "I know," he insisted, "that my Redeemer lives!"

In the end, Job held tightly to his love and faith in God. Job pleased God by his patience in suffering. So the Lord showed that He was pleased with him by rewarding him. He restored Job's health and doubled his wealth, and gave him seven more sons and three more daughters.

Sometimes when we suffer pain or sorrow, we may feel as if God is punishing us. When difficult times surround us, we may wonder why God is putting us through such anguish.

During such hard times, do we have the faith of Job, or do we blame the Lord? We should remember Job's example, and pray that we can have the faith he had.

Next, we'll meet Jonah, who had his own difficulties, of an unusual kind: He found himself in the belly of a huge fish! But unlike Job, Jonah was personally responsible for his predicament, because he had tried to run away from the call of God.

Jonah and the Great Fish

Nineveh was the great city of the Assyrians. Its inhabitants worshiped false gods, and they were brutal and wicked.

One day, the Lord spoke to Jonah, a prophet. "Go to Nineveh, that great city, and cry against it," God commanded; "for their wickedness has come up before me."

But Jonah was afraid of the cruel Assyrians. So he tried to flee from God's presence. He boarded a ship that was bound for a city located in the opposite direction.

The Lord knew exactly were Jonah was. So He sent a great storm across the sea, and the ship was in danger of being destroyed. The men cried out to their gods for help.

The shipmaster found Jonah fast asleep. He woke him and told him to get out of bed. "Call upon your god!" he insisted. "Perhaps the god will give a thought to us, that we do not perish!"

Jonah finally admitted that God had sent the storm because of the prophet's disobedience. He said, "Take me up and throw me into the sea; then the sea will quiet down for you; for I know it is because of me that this great tempest has come upon you."

The crew was reluctant to throw Jonah overboard. But the storm only grew more fierce, threatening to drown them all. So at last they did as Jonah had told them. They cast him into the sea—and the sea became calm.

The Lord then sent a great fish to swallow Jonah, and Jonah remained in the belly of the fish for three days and three nights. He prayed to the Lord to be rescued, and God caused the fish to cast him up on the shore.

A second time God spoke to Jonah. "Go to Nineveh, that great city," He instructed, "and proclaim to it the message that I tell you."

This time Jonah obeyed. He went to Nineveh as the Lord had instructed him. When he entered the city, he cried out, "Yet forty days, and Nineveh shall be overthrown!"

The people of Nineveh believed that Jonah was a messenger from God. They began a great fast to show that they were sorry for their wickedness. The king and all the people, from the greatest to the least, put on sackcloth and did penance. They even put sackcloth on their animals! When God saw that they wanted to repent and change their ways, He had mercy and spared them.

When we think about the story of Jonah, we may be tempted to focus on his unusual adventure inside the great fish. But this is much more than an unforgettable fish story! What happened to Jonah teaches us several important lessons.

First, Jonah's story shows us that we can't run away from God.

Second, it shows that God loves everyone, even those who don't know Him or obey Him. He wants them to be saved from the consequences of their sins.

Finally, Jonah's story shows us that God is merciful. He's pleased when we turn away from sin, and He forgives us.

This story will come up again in the Gospels of the New Testament. There, Jesus foretells His own resurrection, saying that just as Jonah was "buried" in the fish's belly for three days, then came out again, Jesus himself will be buried in the earth, then rise again the third day. Jonah's experience is yet one more foreshadowing of things to come.

PART FIVE
How God's People Went Into
Exile and Returned

CHAPTER 18

The Assyrian Invasions

The Assyrians Attack Israel
For a while the kingdoms of Judah and of Israel were prosperous. They continued to regain the territory that their enemies had taken from them. They rebuilt their cities, and they constructed forts in the deserts and open countries to protect themselves from invasions.

The wealthy people of the two kingdoms amassed fine jewelry and other luxuries. The prophets tell about their expensive stone houses and ivory couches, and their harps and other musical instruments. They had an abundance of wine, oil, meats, and other fine foods.

But we also learn from the prophets, and especially from the prophets Amos and Hosea, that the poor were oppressed by the rich. They were treated cruelly and forced to work hard for little pay. The prophets, the great men of God, rebuked the people for this mistreatment, and also for their idolatry, dishonesty, murder, and adultery. They foretold that both kingdoms would face disaster because of all this wickedness.

The disaster soon came. First, there was a rebellion on the part of the poor and downtrodden. Then, the Assyrians invaded the land, and all prosperity came to an end.

Assyria was a growing nation. The king of Israel tried to gain the friendship of the Assyrian king by offering gifts of great value. He even promised to pay tribute to him and to be his faithful ally, hoping to convince the Assyrians not to invade their land.

But the sins and idolatry of Israel had to be punished. So God allowed the king of Assyria to invade the Kingdom of Israel and destroy the capital city of Samaria. The king was thrown into prison and the Samaritans were taken prisoner. They were brought far away to Assyria and made to settle in Media, in the eastern part of the country.

The Noble Tobit

Tobit belonged to the tribe of Naphtali. He was one of the Samaritans who were taken captive to Media after the invasion of the Assyrians. Tobit had never taken part in idolatry as many of his people did, when they adored the golden calves set up in his country. He remained obedient to the law that commanded the Israelites to worship in Jerusalem. Even while he was a prisoner in Media, he obeyed the Law of Moses, which forbade the people to eat certain kinds of food.

The king of Assyria was cruel to the captives in Media. Many were put to death, and their bodies were left to rot in the streets. Tobit went out of his way to bury the dead and gave help to their needy relatives.

The king heard of Tobit's kindness and was enraged by his simple acts of charity. He ordered that Tobit be put to death. But Tobit escaped and fled from the land, hiding himself until after the king had died.

Under the new king, the Israelites enjoyed more liberty and freedom. Tobit returned and was able to live a normal life again, continuing with his works of charity. One night, after a hard day of labor, he lay on the ground beside the wall of his courtyard, and he rested.

While he was lying there, the droppings from birds sitting above him on a wall fell into his eyes and blinded him. As a blind man, he was unable to work as he had before, so he became poor. His family's only income was from the work his wife did as a weaver of cloth.

Toward the end of his life, when Tobit believed that death was near, he called for his son, Tobias. Then he gave him these words of wisdom:

"My son, when I die, bury me, and do not neglect your mother. Honor her all the days of your life; do what is pleasing to her, and do not grieve her. Remember, my son, that she faced many dangers for you while you were yet unborn. When she dies, bury her beside me in the same grave.

"Remember the Lord our God all your days, my son, and refuse to sin or to transgress His commandments. Live uprightly all the days of your life, and do not walk in the ways of wrongdoing. For if you do what is true, your ways will prosper through your deeds.

"Give alms from your possessions to all who live uprightly, and do not let your eye begrudge the gift when you make it. Do not turn your face away from any poor man, and the face of God will not be turned away from you.

"If you have many possessions, make your gift from them in proportion; if few, do not be afraid to give according to the little you have. . . . For charity delivers from death and keeps you from entering the darkness; and for all who practice it charity is an excellent offering in the presence of the Most High."

Then Tobit thought of some money he had lent to his friend Gabael in the city of Rages years before, when he had been rich and before he went blind. Tobit told his son to seek out a faithful man as a companion to go with him to collect the debt from Gabael.

Tobias Accompanied by a Special Guide

Young Tobias prepared for the journey, but before leaving he followed his father's advice to seek out a faithful man to join him. He found a young stranger in the city and requested his services as a guide. The man agreed, and they set out on the journey together.

On the way, they came to a river. Tobias went to wash his feet, and as he did, a monstrous fish leapt out of the water to devour him. His companion told him to catch the fish by the gills and pull it ashore. Then he instructed him to cut out the heart, the gall, and the liver, and to save them for medicine. When Tobias asked his guide what they were good for, the guide told him that the gall was good for anointing and curing eyes.

Tobias was led by his guide to a distant relative, whose daughter, Sarah, he married. Sarah's father gave her and Tobias, as a wedding present, one half of his property, with the promise that they would inherit the rest when he died.

The wedding feast lasted two weeks. Tobias was unable to leave, for it wouldn't have been right to abandon

his bride. So the guide set out alone to collect the debt from Gabael. He found him and collected the money, then invited Gabael to come back with him to the feast.

After the feast, Tobias, Sarah, and the guide set out for home. When they arrived, Tobias recalled that the guide had claimed the gall they retrieved from the fish was good for anointing and curing eyes. So Tobias ran to his blind father and placed the gall in his eyes as a salve. Tobit immediately recovered his sight!

When Tobit and his son sought to pay the guide for his great services, he revealed his identity. The guide said, "I am Raphael, one of the seven holy angels who present the prayers of the saints and enter into the presence of the glory of the Lord."

In fear, they all fell on their faces, but the angel said, "Do not be afraid; you will be safe. But praise God for ever. For I did not come as a favor on my part, but by the will of our God."

The angel assured Tobit that he had seen all the good deeds he had done in his life, and that he had been sent to Tobit to cure him because of all these good deeds. When the men stood up again, the angel had disappeared.

After prophesying about events to come, the old man Tobit died at a good old age.

There may be no one nobler in the Old Testament than the man Tobit. He courageously practiced charity and showed respect for the dead when he buried those who had been killed by the cruel king. He graciously accepted the will of God when he became blind, without blaming God for this misfortune. In his touching message to Tobias, his son, he urged him to respect his mother, give to the poor, and listen to the word of God.

In all these ways, Tobit serves as a model for living an honorable and noble life. In addition, when Tobit's story comes to an end, God shows us that He will reward such virtues.

Next, we'll meet a good king who respected the Lord, another great prophet, and a fearless woman who saved her people through her courage and wit.

Hezekiah, King of Judah, and the Prophet Isaiah

At the time the Samaritans were taken captive by the Assyrian king, a man named Hezekiah ruled over the Kingdom of Judah. When he was only twenty-four years old he had been made king. He was a holy man and listened to the prophets of God.

Hezekiah destroyed all the shrines where idols were worshiped and tore down all the altars that had been built outside Jerusalem in defiance of the Law. At his command the priests and Levites cleansed the Temple and removed an altar that had been placed there in honor of the false gods. Seven days were spent in purifying the Temple.

Hezekiah also restored the order of the services as they had existed in the time of David. He provided the animals for the sacrifices of the morning and evening of each day, and for the feast days prescribed by the Law of Moses. He urged the people to pay the priests the first fruits and tithes as required in the Law of Moses, and the people obeyed him.

Once Hezekiah became terribly sick, almost to the point of death. Isaiah, one of the greatest prophets in the Old Testament, came to him and said, "Thus says the Lord: Set your house in order; for you shall die, you shall not recover."

When Hezekiah heard this frightening message, he turned his face to the wall and prayed to the Lord, saying, "Remember now, O Lord, . . . how I have walked before You in faithfulness and with a whole heart, and have done what is good in Your sight." Then Hezekiah wept.

Isaiah was just about to leave when he heard the voice of the Lord, urging him to tell Hezekiah that He had heard his prayer. The Lord, after seeing the king's tears, promised to extend Hezekiah's life by fifteen more years. Then the Lord promised to deliver him and his people from the assault of the Assyrians.

For a time, Hezekiah followed the advice of the prophet Isaiah by putting his trust in the power of God. But later, he acted contrary to Isaiah's advice and put his trust in the Egyptians instead. He formed an alliance with Egypt and defied the Assyrians, who were ruled by the cruel and proud king Sennacherib.

This king marched westward with his armies, conquering the Phoenicians, the Amorites, the Moabites, and the Edomites. He captured cities that belonged to the Philistines and the Kingdom of Judah. As he was surrounding the city of Lachish, in Judah, Hezekiah offered him an enormous tribute if he would leave the country.

Sennacherib withdrew, but he returned in a short time. Twice he sent messengers to demand the surrender of Jerusalem. Isaiah the prophet encouraged the people to stand firm against the enemy, and Hezekiah begged God to deliver him from this evil Sennacherib.

Hezekiah's trust in God would save him.

That night, an angel entered the camp of the Assyrians and killed one hundred and eighty-five thousand soldiers. Sennacherib was so frightened by the slaughter that he returned to Assyria, never again coming after the Kingdom of Judah.

Hezekiah went on to do many good things in the extra years the Lord gave him. He recaptured the cities that had been taken from his father by the Philistines, strengthened the fortifications of his kingdom, improved the defenses of Jerusalem, and provided a water supply for the city.

Judith Saves the Kingdom
After Hezekiah, his wicked son Manasseh became king of Judah. When the Assyrians made a second attack on that kingdom, Jerusalem was captured and Manasseh was led away as a prisoner to Babylon.

Holofernes, an Assyrian general, had an enormous army of one hundred and twenty thousand footmen and twenty thousand horsemen. He attacked the city of Bethulia. The people defended the city bravely, but when the Assyrians cut off their water supply, they begged their leader to surrender. They could not survive without

their water, so they held a council of war and decided that, if no help came within five days, they would give up the city.

Suddenly, a woman spoke up to rebuke the elders of the city for putting a time limit on the power of God. She was angered that they would test God this way. Her name was Judith, and she was a rich, beautiful, and virtuous widow of the city of Bethulia.

Judith promised to put an end to the battle. She prayed for success and then set out to visit the Assyrian camp. She was brought before the general Holofernes.

Judith told him that she fled from the city to escape the inevitable attack of his cruel soldiers. Instead of being a victim of his attack, she wanted to flee and find him, and tell him the best routes into the city where he could overcome them without losing a single soldier. Holofernes was pleased with her and gave her and her maids a tent.

Four days later, Holofernes hosted a great feast for his officers and invited Judith. At the feast, Holofernes became drunk with wine and fell into a deep sleep. The officers left him alone in his tent. Judith then took the sword of Holofernes, cut off his head, hid it in a pouch, and hurried to Bethulia.

When she returned, the people were shocked at her bravery and welcomed her with great joy. At daybreak, the soldiers of the town attacked the Assyrians. But the enemy was panic-stricken when they discovered that their leader had been killed in the night. So they fled to the hills, and the people of Judah followed them and defeated the invaders.

Later, Manasseh their king was released, and so ended this campaign against Judah.

Once again, God used people of good faith and courage to show us how He rewards trust in Him. It seemed as if all would be lost for Hezekiah in his battles with the Assyrians. But in the middle of the night an angel came and destroyed his enemy. Meanwhile, a faithful woman such as Judith, who loved God dearly, saved her kingdom with a clever strategy and a remarkable bravery.

Nevertheless, despite the wisdom of Isaiah, the faith of Hezekiah, and the courage of Judith, soon their people would again be captives in a foreign land.

CHAPTER 19

Daniel and the Babylonian Captivity

Attacks on Jerusalem and the Warnings of Jeremiah

Egypt and Babylonia were now at war with each other. In Judah, the people were divided: One group favored Egypt, while the other favored Babylonia. Jehoiakim was king at the time, and Jeremiah, the priest and prophet, warned him to obey God and to trust in Him rather than trust in an alliance with the king of Egypt.

Jeremiah prophesied the evils that would come to the people of Judah if they relied on Egypt. Since Jehoiakim favored the Egyptians, he ordered Jeremiah's arrest. The prophet was imprisoned several times. Once he was even thrown down into a hole where rainwater was stored, and he sank in the mud there up to his knees.

But Jeremiah's enemies could not silence him as he spoke God's message to the people. His words were soon fulfilled.

Nebuchadnezzar, son of the king of Babylon, attacked Jerusalem because of its alliance with Egypt. He captured the city and took many of the men there as captives. He carried off the sacred vessels of the Temple and put King Jehoiakim in prison. After a short time in prison, Jehoiakim was released and restored to his throne, but only because he was made to swear allegiance to the king of Babylon and become his subject.

Three years later, Jehoiakim rebelled against the Babylonians. But the Babylonian army entered Jerusalem to put down his rebellion, and he and his men were killed. The city was conquered and the son of Jehoiakim was placed on the throne in his place.

After three months, Nebuchadnezzar himself came to Jerusalem, still angry about the rebellion. He burned the Temple and carried off the king and his family. He took with him seven thousand Jewish soldiers and every skilled workman he could find. Then he placed on the throne of Judah as his subject the uncle of the king, whom he named Zedekiah.

For a time, Zedekiah listened to Jeremiah, asking for his counsel and even for the prayers of the man of God. So Jeremiah enjoyed freedom under Zedekiah. He walked the streets of the city with a yoke on his neck as a warning of what was in store for the people if they continued their wicked lives and their trust in Egypt, rather than in God. He wrote letters to those already taken captive and urged them to be patient and to await the time when they would be free.

After a while, however, Zedekiah no longer listened to Jeremiah. He joined the Egyptians against the Babylonians. Nebuchadnezzar came to Jerusalem for the fourth time to attack. During the siege, Jeremiah preached in the city and told the people that all who joined Nebuchadnezzar and the Babylonians would be saved. For this message, he was cast into prison.

The siege of the city continued for two years. Finally, a breach was made in the walls, and the city was taken by the Babylonians. Zedekiah fled, but the enemy pursued and captured him. He and his children were brought to Nebuchadnezzar. His children were put to death right in front of him, then his eyes were plucked out, and he was taken as a prisoner to Babylon.

Everything of value was taken from the houses of Jerusalem. The important buildings were destroyed, including the beautiful Temple that Solomon had built. Even the walls of the city were torn down. But Jeremiah was spared and allowed to remain in Jerusalem.

While the Babylonians were plundering the city and before they reached the Temple, Jeremiah and some Levites secretly removed the Ark of the Covenant and the altar of incense. They carried them across the Jordan and hid them in a cave in Mount Nebo. The place where they hid them was not marked in any special way, so the treasure would not be found by the enemy.

The sad sight of Jerusalem in ruins inspired Jeremiah to write the Book of Lamentations. This biblical book is filled with bitter cries of grief over the ruin of God's people, their land, their capital city, and their Temple.

Once again, the people of God had fallen on hard times because of their sin and their failure to trust God. They were taken off to a distant land where they were made to live, in most regards, like slaves. But God had not forgotten them, and His plan was to send yet another holy man among them to restore their faith—a man who could stand up to injustice, defy hungry lions, interpret dreams, and lead his people to better times.

The Stories of Daniel

After the final attack on Jerusalem by the Babylonians, the captives from Judah were sent to Babylon and the neighboring country. Babylon had been attacked and conquered many times in the past, leaving it in ruins. So it had to be entirely rebuilt.

Nebuchadnezzar had a plan. He decided to use the skilled laborers among the Judean prisoners he had brought back with him to rebuild his country. He forced them to work very hard for days on end. They repaired the old city wall of Babylon and built a second outer wall. They dug a canal connecting the Tigris and the Euphrates rivers a short distance north of Babylon, and they restored nearly all the Babylonian cities.

The Judeans who belonged to the noble families were treated more kindly. Among these were a man named Daniel and his three friends, Hananiah, Mishael, and Azariah. They were cared for and educated as members of the king's own family. The prophet Ezekiel was also given great freedom. He went about and encouraged the Jews (as the Judeans came to be known) to trust in God to deliver them from captivity.

Daniel Saves Susanna

While the Jews were in captivity, they were governed by elders of their own people. These elders often came to the house of a man named Joakim and his wife, Susanna, to judge the cases brought to them by the people. Susanna was a very beautiful woman who honored the Lord.

One day, when the people had left the house, Susanna walked in her husband's orchard alone. She didn't know it, but hiding in the orchard were two of the elders, who lusted after her beauty.

224

When they saw her alone, they came out from their hiding place and tried to convince her to sin against her husband. But Susanna turned her back on them and refused. So the elders threatened to tell a terrible lie about her: that she had been cheating on her husband with another man. They claimed they would spread this false rumor to the people so that she would be condemned to death for the crime.

Susanna was in a terribly difficult position. If she gave in to these wicked men, she would be sinning against the Lord. But if she refused them, they would spread lies that would lead to her death and her family's dishonor.

She sighed deeply and told the elders: "I am hemmed in on every side. For if I do this thing, it is death for me; and if I do not, I shall not escape your hands. I choose not to do it and to fall into your hands, rather than to sin in the sight of the Lord."

After she refused their advances, Susanna cried out for help, bringing her servants into the garden where Susanna and the two men were. But the men cried out against Susanna, accusing her of a sin she didn't commit.

The next day the council of elders met in her very own house, for her husband was one of the elders who ruled on such cases. The panel heard the two elders say that they had seen Susanna with another man, and when they confronted them, the man ran away. The panel condemned her to death after hearing the false story.

Everyone there, including her parents, her husband, and all her friends, believed that she was guilty. After all, it was two elders of the city who were accusing her, and they were greatly respected by all the people.

Susanna wept and looked up to heaven, for her heart had confidence in the Lord. She prayed, "O eternal God, who discern what is secret, who are aware of all things before they come to be, You know that these men have borne false witness against me. And now I am to die! Yet I have done none of the things that they have wickedly invented against me!"

She didn't know it at the time, but the Lord heard her cry.

When she was led out to be put to death, the Lord spoke to Daniel, who cried out to the people: "Are you such fools, you sons of Israel? Have you condemned a daughter of Israel without examination and without learning the facts? Return to the place of judgment. For these men have borne false witness against her."

Daniel had a plan to reveal what had really happened. He would separate the two men who had accused Susanna, then ask each of them alone what had happened. If their stories matched, it would be clear that they were telling the truth about the wrong Susanna had done. But if their stories differed, then they were clearly lying, for if they both witnessed the same event, they should tell the same story.

So Daniel separated the two men and questioned each one without the other. He asked under which tree they had seen Susanna cheating on her husband. The first elder answered that he saw her and the man under a mastic tree; the second elder said that he had seen them under an oak.

Daniel declared their crime before the people, and he told the two men that God's judgment would lead to their death.

When the assembly had heard Daniel's judgment, they praised God for saving those who trust in Him. They rose up against the elders and put them to death. Then Daniel became a highly respected leader among the people from that day forward.

Daniel and the King's Dreams
One day, King Nebuchadnezzar had a dream that frightened him. But as often happens with dreams, once he awoke, he couldn't remember what the dream was about. He remembered that it had been a terrifying nightmare, but he couldn't remember why it was so terrifying.

Nebuchadnezzar called together all the wise men and magicians within his kingdom to find among them one who could both tell him what he had dreamed and explain the meaning of it. But no one could be found to do such a difficult thing. In his frustration and fury, the king ordered all the wise men in Babylon to be put to death.

When Daniel heard what had happened, he begged God to reveal the secret of the king's dream, so that lives could be spared. God heard him and revealed the dream to Daniel that night in a vision.

The next day, Daniel went before the king and said that God had given him the power to reveal the forgotten dream to him. Daniel claimed it was the one true God, and that God alone, who reveals deep and hidden things and knows what is in darkness. Then Daniel described the dream, and explained how it was a dream of things to come.

When the king heard Daniel's explanation of the dream, it all came back to him. Everything Daniel had said was right.

Nebuchadnezzar cried out, "Truly, your God is God of gods and Lord of kings, and a revealer of mysteries, for you have been able to reveal this mystery."

He promoted Daniel to the position of governor over all the provinces of Babylon, and chief of all the wise men in his kingdom. He placed the companions of Daniel in charge of the city's buildings and works.

The burdens of the Jewish workers were lightened by their new governor. They began to receive payment for their labor and were then able to buy their freedom. They settled in colonies and began to engage in farming and other business pursuits. They were kept from idolatry by the courage of Daniel and other strong leaders among them who led them to God.

During this time, the priests and Levites instructed the Jews in the Law and counseled them. They couldn't offer sacrifices as they had done in Jerusalem, but they offered prayers in the morning, at noon, and in the evening. They had no Temple, but they built *synagogues*, assembly halls where they gathered to worship God and listen to readings from their sacred writings.

In short, life became much better for the Jews living in Babylon, despite their captivity and their exile from their homeland. The city eventually became a great center of Jewish learning.

Daniel's Companions in the Fiery Furnace

Some of the leading men of Babylon were jealous of Daniel's young friends Hananiah, Mishael, and Azariah, whom they called Shadrach, Meshach, and Abednego. These three were foreigners living in their land, yet the king had placed them in high-ranking positions. So the Babylonian leaders looked for a way to get rid of these young men.

When Nebuchadnezzar erected a great golden idol and demanded that all the people worship it, the leading men of Babylon knew their opportunity had come. The king commanded all the chief men of the provinces to come to Babylon and offer sacrifice to the statue. But Daniel's three friends refused to obey that command.

Someone reported to the king that Shadrach, Meshach,

and Abednego were absent from the assembly to worship the statue. The king was furious. He commanded the three young men to be bound and thrown into a blazing furnace to be burned alive.

Then an amazing thing happened that those who were watching could hardly believe. God sent an angel to protect Daniel's three friends. Their bonds were burned away, but they themselves were shielded from the flames. They walked around freely inside the furnace, proclaiming their love for God.

Abednego cried out a prayer of thanks to the Lord while he stood surrounded by the flames. He prayed: "Blessed are You, O Lord, God of our fathers, and worthy of praise; and Your name is glorified forever. For You are just in all that You have done to us, and all Your works are true and Your ways right, and all Your judgments are truth."

When Nebuchadnezzar himself saw the three men walking around inside the furnace, untouched by the fire, he was astounded. He called them out of the furnace, and all who were there saw that they had no burns on their bodies. So the king blessed them and their God, and threatened any man who spoke out against them and their God.

Daniel in the Lions' Den

One of Nebuchadnezzar's successors was a man named King Darius. He made Daniel one of the three presidents who ruled over all the other officials of the land. Darius was so impressed with Daniel's performance that he planned to give him authority over the entire kingdom.

Once again, the Babylonian officials grew jealous and angry that a Jewish man would be placed over them. Worse yet, Daniel had demonstrated to the king that the priests of the Babylonian god Bel were frauds. So the prophet had many enemies, and they sought to bring some charge against him.

Daniel was blameless in performing his duties, so they couldn't accuse him of any wrongdoing in his public service. But they knew that Daniel carefully obeyed the laws that God had given to the Jewish people. So they found a way to trap him.

The Babylonian officials persuaded Darius to make a new law: For thirty days, no one was to make a petition to anyone, whether a man or a god, except Darius himself. That meant they were forbidden even to pray! If they did, they would be thrown into a den of hungry lions.

The officials knew that Daniel prayed faithfully three times a day. They also knew that he would disobey the king's command in order to follow the Law of God. So they spied on him, and when they found him praying, they went to the king, demanding that Daniel be put to death as the new law required.

The officials threatened to revolt and kill the king if he didn't sentence Daniel to death. They even accused him of having become a Jew and forsaking the gods of Babylon. In fear, the king gave in to their demands. He commanded that Daniel be arrested and thrown into a den of hungry lions.

Darius had been reluctant to act against Daniel. He had great respect for the prophet and his God, and he realized that he had acted foolishly when he made the law against praying. So as the prophet was being dragged off, the king said to him, "May your God, whom you serve continually, deliver you!"

For six days the lions received no food, because the Babylonians were hoping to starve them. That way, their great hunger would drive them to rip Daniel apart right away.

But Daniel remained firm, placing his trust in God. And when he was thrown into the lions' den, his faith

was rewarded: Despite their hunger, the lions refused to harm him. God had sent an angel to protect Daniel.

At that time, back in the land of Judah there was a prophet named Habakkuk. He had just prepared a meal when an angel appeared. The angel instructed him to take some of the dinner to Babylon, and give it to Daniel in the lions' den.

Habakkuk protested that he had never been to Babylon and knew nothing about the lions' den. So the angel carried him to Babylon, right to the den, so he could give Daniel the food. Then the angel carried him back home.

The next morning, Darius came to find out what had happened to the prophet. He shouted into the den, "O Daniel, servant of the living God, has your God, whom you serve continually, been able to deliver you from the lions?"

Daniel shouted back, "My God sent his angel and shut the lions' mouths, and they have not hurt me, because I was found blameless before him; and before you, O king, I have done no wrong."

When the king learned that Daniel had not been harmed by the lions, he commanded that the prophet be released. Then he commanded that those who had unjustly persecuted Daniel should suffer the same fate they had intended for the prophet. The Babylonian leaders were cast into the very same den of lions. Immediately, the hungry beasts devoured them.

Daniel Reads the Handwriting on the Wall

After the reign of King Darius, the kings of Babylon were usurpers who had no right to the throne. Daniel's influence with them was not very strong, though he was not entirely forgotten.

Belshazzar, one of these kings, made a great feast one night and invited a thousand of his nobles. As they dined on delicious food, the king commanded his servants to bring the vessels of gold and silver that Nebuchadnezzar had stolen from the Temple in Jerusalem years ago. He wanted everyone to drink from them. But these were sacred vessels dedicated to God, and they were not to be used this way.

Still, the vessels were brought into the banquet hall and filled with wine. Then the king and all his guests drank from them in honor of their false gods.

Suddenly, the fingers of a man's hand appeared from nowhere and began to write on the wall!

When the king saw this apparition, he was terrified. He grew pale, his knees knocked together, and he nearly fainted! Though he tried to read the words that the mysterious fingers were writing, he couldn't make them out. So he sent for his wise men, magicians, and astrologers.

The king promised that whoever would read the writing and interpret it for him would be clothed with purple and have a golden chain on his neck. In addition, the interpreter would be ranked as the third man in the kingdom. But not one of the wise men, magicians, or astrologers could read the writing, nor tell what it meant.

The king became more and more terrified. His guests, too, were greatly troubled. Then the queen advised Belshazzar to send for Daniel.

Daniel was brought to the banquet room, and the king said to him, "You are that Daniel, one of the exiles of Judah, whom the king my father brought from Judah. I have heard of you that the spirit of the holy God is in you, and that light and understanding and excellent wisdom are found in you. . . . Now if you can read the writing and make known to me its interpretation, you shall be clothed with purple, and have a chain of gold about your neck, and shall be the third ruler in the kingdom."

Daniel replied, "Let your gifts be for yourself, and give your rewards to another; nevertheless I will read the writing to the king and make known to him the interpretation."

The prophet then called on God to help him interpret the strange writing on the wall. Through God, Daniel told all who were present that the writing was a warning. It meant that all who were there would be punished for drinking wine from the sacred vessels that had come from the Temple in Jerusalem. The people known as the Medes and the Persians, Daniel prophesied, would invade and overcome them.

Daniel's prophecy was fulfilled that very night. The Persians turned the course of the Euphrates River and entered the city by way of the river bed. Belshazzar was put to death by the invaders and, after a short battle, the Babylonian army surrendered. Darius the Mede became king.

We often look to Daniel as a model for having faith in God even when we face terrifying situations. But Daniel should be remembered for much more than his hours in the lions' den. He was a great symbol of hope for the Jews during their captivity in Babylon. While there, through the help and inspiration of Daniel, God's people were actually able to flourish, even though they were in exile.

Next, we'll learn more about these great men called the prophets, who keep showing up in the Old Testament stories. Who exactly were these men, and why they were so important in God's plan?

CHAPTER 20

The Prophets

The Life of Prophets

We usually think of a prophet as a man who foretells some future event. The prophets whose writings are found in the Bible are indeed the holy men who foretold the future, especially the coming of the Savior. Yet predicting the future was only a part of the work of a prophet among the Jews.

The prophet was looked on as the messenger of God, who spoke for God among His people. He not only foretold the future; he also told the people what they must do to please God at the present time.

The prophets often lived apart from the people, very much like members of religious orders today, such as monks living in a monastery. Whoever wanted to become a prophet usually took part in a special course of training. There were schools of prophets, where many of these holy men studied, though not all of them were prepared to preach the word of God. Then they went out as missionaries among the people.

The Bible contains the writings of only a few of the prophets. But there were many who had great influence with the people, such as Samuel in the days of Saul, Nathan in the days of David, and Elijah in the reign of Ahab. From the very beginning, God sent these holy guides to reveal His holy will to His chosen people.

The prophets whose writings have been preserved are divided into two classes: the *major* prophets and the *minor* prophets. The major prophets are those whose works take up a large part of the Bible. The writings of the minor prophets fill only a few pages each.

The major prophets are *Isaiah, Jeremiah, Ezekiel* and *Daniel.* Let's take a closer look now at their ministries.

Isaiah, "The Great Prophet"
Very little is known about the prophet Isaiah. According to the tradition of the Jews, he belonged to the royal family, and his writings show that he was an educated man. An ancient tradition says that he suffered martyrdom at the hands of a wicked king.

Isaiah lived in the days before the people of Judah were taken away into captivity. The mighty nation of the Assyrians was threatening them on one side, while the Egyptians closed in on them from the other side. The Kingdoms of Israel and of Judah had fallen away from God and no longer looked to Him for protection. They sought safety in their own strength, or in treaties with earthly powers.

Isaiah prophesied to the people and told them not to fear their enemies. He urged them to put their trust in God, who had saved them in the past and would save them in the future. But he knew the people wouldn't listen to him. They would follow their own ways, and one day they would be carried away into captivity and death.

But even when they were taken captive, Isaiah prophesied, God would deliver them. First, an earthly king would set them free. This king was Cyrus, the Persian ruler. Then years later, Isaiah predicted, the Great Deliverer, whom the Jews called the *Messiah,* would save the whole world.

Isaiah is known as "the Great Prophet" because of the wonderful things he foretold. He predicted, in beautiful poetry, the coming of Christ, the bitter passion and death of our Savior, and the establishment of the Church.

Centuries before the birth of Christ, Isaiah said: "Therefore the Lord himself will give you a sign. Behold, a virgin shall conceive and bear a son, and shall call his name Immanuel. . . . For to us a child is born, to us a son is given; and the government will be upon his shoulder, and his name will be called 'Wonderful Counselor, Mighty God, Everlasting Father, Prince of Peace.'"

The name "Immanuel" means "God with us." With these words, Isaiah was prophesying that Christ would be born to the Virgin Mary, and He would save us all.

Isaiah also prophesied about the sufferings our Savior would endure. He said: "He was wounded for our transgressions, he was bruised for our iniquities; upon him was the chastisement that made us whole, and with his stripes we are healed."

Isaiah also told how Christ would go willingly to his death on our behalf: "He was oppressed, and he was afflicted, yet he opened not his mouth; like a lamb that is led to the slaughter, and like a sheep that before its shearers is silent, so he opened not his mouth."

Isaiah also foretold that the Church of Christ would draw the people to herself. All nations would flow to His Church, and the peoples would be converted to God.

The Prophet Jeremiah

It was about the year 586 B.C. that the Jews were carried off into captivity by the Babylonians. For forty years the prophet Jeremiah had been warning them that this terrible punishment would come upon them unless they repented of their sins and returned to God. But they refused to listen to him.

The terrible day came, and we have already seen how the king of Judah, all the nobility, the people, and the vessels of the Temple were carried off by the king of Babylon.

Jeremiah was left behind in the ruins of the Temple and the city to mourn for his people. As we have noted, it was then that he wrote the Book of Lamentations, one of the most beautiful books in the Bible. It describes the destruction of Jerusalem and the great suffering of the people.

The heart of Jeremiah is bowed down with grief and loneliness. Yet he doesn't lose his hope in God. He knows that the day will come when God will deliver His people from bondage.

The Prophet Ezekiel

Ezekiel was among those who had been carried away from Jerusalem by the Babylonians. He prophesied for many years after the death of Jeremiah. He addressed his message not only to the Jews who were left behind in Jerusalem, but also to those who were in captivity. His message is one of hope and of victory, saying that God will be true to His promises and deliver His people from the hand of the enemy.

Ezekiel prophesied in parables, or short symbolic stories, which are sometimes hard to understand. In one vision, for example, he saw a great whirlwind and a great cloud surrounded by fire. In the midst of the cloud and fire he saw what looked like four living creatures: a man, a lion, an ox, and an eagle.

The symbols of the four Evangelists, or Gospel writers, come from this vision. St. Matthew is represented as a man, St. Mark as a lion, St. Luke as an ox, and St. John as an eagle.

The Prophet Daniel

We've seen how Daniel lived in Babylon during the captivity, and how he received the gift of wisdom from God. This gift made him a favorite with the king, who treated him as though he were a prince. Even after the fall of Babylon, when the Medes and Persians came into power, Daniel remained in authority.

Daniel told the people constantly that even though they were captives in the hands of a mighty nation, they should not lose hope. God had not forgotten His promises and was watching over them. He foretold the time of their deliverance and the coming of the Savior.

These prophets, and all the other prophets of the Bible, knew the mind of God in many ways. The Lord speaks to us still today through their words. If we read the prophets and listen to Him speaking, we too can know more about God and His will for our lives.

CHAPTER 21

The Return to Jerusalem

The Decree of Cyrus

The empire ruled by Cyrus reached from the Mediterranean Sea all the way to Persia (the land we now call Iran). But Egypt was not part of his empire. Cyrus saw that it would be to his advantage to have a friendly nation between himself and Egypt.

With this purpose in mind, Cyrus issued a decree that permitted all the Jews from the Kingdom of Judah to return there. He gave back to them the sacred vessels that had been taken from the Temple by King Nebuchadnezzar. And he gave orders for the Temple to be rebuilt.

The Jews had been captives in Babylon for seventy years. During these years, the Assyrians and Babylonians had ruled over the land of Judah through a governor whom they appointed from a neighboring province.

Most of the Jews had managed to support themselves very well in Babylon and had established homes there.

They were afraid to risk the dangers of a journey to Judah, so they decided to remain in Babylon. Though they and their descendants had come to Babylon as prisoners, they had made themselves a home there over the decades, and they weren't ready to leave.

For this reason, only about forty-two thousand, three hundred and sixty Jews returned to their own country in Judah. The majority of these were people of great faith. But there were also some lazy people, and others who were merely looking for adventure.

The leader of the returning exiles of Judah was a man named Zerubbabel. He belonged to the family of the kings of Judah, but he had never seen Jerusalem. He came as the representative of the Persian king and as governor of the province. Joshua, the high priest, accompanied him.

Meanwhile, the people who had been taken captive from the northern kingdom of Israel never returned to their country as a people. They had been in captivity more than two hundred years, and they had scattered to several faraway nations. They had no religious leadership, and they had largely forgotten their native land.

The Return to Jerusalem and the Rebuilding of the Temple

The journey from Babylon to Jerusalem took seven months. As soon as the Jews reached the city, they built an altar for the morning and evening sacrifices. The sacrifices for the great feasts of the Jews were also offered on this altar.

Preparations for rebuilding the Temple were made in the second year after their return to Jerusalem. Laying the foundational stone was a solemn occasion. The priests, dressed in their robes, played on their trumpets, and the people sang songs of joy.

Some of the neighboring people offered to help in the building of the Temple. They claimed to worship the God of Israel along with their own gods. But the Jews believed that it wouldn't be right for idol-worshippers to take part in building the Temple of the one true God. So they turned down the offer.

This refusal made the idolaters angry. They sent word to the king of Persia that the Jews were building the Temple as a fortress to resist him. The king believed this report, and he ordered the governor of Samaria to prevent the completion of the Temple.

At this time the prophets Haggai and Zechariah urged the people to continue building the Temple, and to keep their faith that all would work out. At last, Darius, who was now king of Persia, listened to the petitions of the Jews. He permitted them to finish the building and gave large sums of money and herds of cattle to promote their worship. It was in the year 515 B.C., twenty years after the first cornerstone had been laid, that the Temple was completed.

Esther Chosen as Queen

After the death of Darius, his son, Ahasuerus, became king of Persia. Wanting to choose a queen, he sent messengers into all the provinces to bring to the palace the most beautiful women in his empire.

Among those brought to the king was a young Jewish woman, an orphan, whose name was Esther. She was accompanied by her uncle, a devout Jew, named Mordecai. He thought that if Esther were made queen, she would be in a position to help her people.

The moment Ahasuerus saw her, he was astounded by her beauty and chose her instantly to be his queen, not knowing that she was a Jew. Mordecai was then given a position in the palace. His duty was to stand at the gates and to see that only those who had permission from the king could enter.

The Devious Haman

The king's chief adviser, a proud and arrogant man named Haman, wanted to overthrow the king. So he entered into a conspiracy with two officers in the king's army. Mordecai discovered the plot, though he didn't know that Haman had taken part in it. Mordecai reported the matter to the king, and the two officers were put to death.

Haman was never suspected in the plot to overthrow the king, but he still hated Mordecai for defeating his plans. Then, at another time, Mordecai refused to bend his knee to Haman in reverence, and so he hated Mordecai all the more.

In order to gain revenge against Mordecai, Haman went to the king and told him that the Jews of his kingdom were preparing to revolt, which was a lie. He advised the king to send out a decree ordering all the Jews to be put to death. Ahasuerus believed Haman's lie, so he sent messengers into every part of his kingdom with orders for all the Jews to be put to death.

When Mordecai heard this terrible news, he told Esther to go before the king and plead for her people. This was a difficult thing for Esther to do, for in those days people didn't approach the king and speak to him unless he invited them to come to him. If anyone broke this rule, they could be put to death. But Esther knew the lives of her people were at stake, and so she decided to approach the king.

Esther told her uncle to call their friends together before the king and have them fast with her for three days and three nights. On the fourth day, she entered the throne room and stood before the king.

Far from being angered at her boldness, the king was pleased with her. He asked her what she wanted and promised to give her even half of his kingdom. Esther told him that she had come to invite him and Haman to a banquet that she had prepared for them that day.

The king came to the banquet, along with Haman. When the king asked to declare her request, she invited them to come again on the following day to a second banquet.

Haman was very proud that he had been invited to eat with the king and the queen. He told his wife and friends that now only one thing was lacking to make him happy. He wanted to see Mordecai dead on a gibbet, where criminals were hung.

Haman's friends advised him to build this gibbet and then ask the king to hang Mordecai on it. So on the very day of the second banquet, Haman built a gibbet and made up his mind to ask the king to condemn Mordecai to death.

That night, the king was restless and couldn't sleep. He called in the historians of his empire, men who had recorded all the events of the previous years, and he commanded them to read aloud the history of his reign. As he listened to the reading, he heard again the story of how Mordecai had uncovered the plot against his life.

The king asked those in his presence whether Mordecai had ever been rewarded for his loyal deed. He was told that Mordecai had never been rewarded at all.

Just then, Haman was in the outer court, about to ask the king to hang Mordecai. When the king saw he was nearby, he summoned Haman and asked, "What shall be done to the man whom the king delights to honor?"

Haman misunderstood what the king was asking. The king was talking about Mordecai, but Haman didn't know that. Instead, Haman thought the king was asking how

Haman himself should be honored. So Haman told the king the kind of grand reward that he hoped to receive.

"For the man whom the king delights to honor," said Haman, "let royal robes be brought, which the king has worn, and the horse which the king has ridden, and on whose head a royal crown is set; and let the robes and the horse be handed over to one of the king's most noble princes; let him array the man whom the king delights to honor, and let him conduct the man on horseback through the open square of the city, proclaiming before him: 'Thus shall it be done to the man whom the king delights to honor.'"

The king very much liked this idea, and for a moment Haman thought he was about to receive such a grand reward. But then the king surprised Haman. He commanded:

"Make haste, take the robes and the horse, as you have said, and do so to Mordecai the Jew who sits at the king's gate. Leave out nothing that you have mentioned."

Haman was furious. Now he had to honor Mordecai, even though he wanted to kill him!

The next day, the king and Haman came to the second banquet that Esther had prepared for them. Again, the king asked her to tell him what she wanted, and he promised again that if she desired it, she could have half of his kingdom.

Instead, Esther pleaded for the life of her people and herself. She claimed that someone had persuaded the king to massacre the Jews by telling lies about them. The king was surprised to hear these words and asked her who had given him the false information.

Esther answered, "A foe and enemy! This wicked Haman!"

Haman was terrified, and rightly so. The king ordered him to be hanged on the same gibbet that he had prepared for Mordecai. The Jews were delivered from death, and Mordecai was given the position that Haman had held.

How ironic! Just as Daniel's persecutors were devoured by the same lions they had prepared for him, so Haman died on the gibbet he had prepared for Mordecai. In each case, wicked people ended up suffering the terrible fate that they had planned for the innocent.

Ezra and Nehemiah

During the reign of Artaxerxes I, there lived in Babylon a Jewish priest whose name was Ezra. He asked the king's permission to gather together as many pilgrims as he could find to return to Jerusalem. The king granted this permission, and at the same time allowed him to take up a collection among the Jews of Babylon. In addition, the king promised to give Ezra a large sum of money, as well as oil and wheat from the revenues that he himself had received from the land of Judah.

The donation that Ezra received from the king was to be used for the restoration of the rites and ceremonies of the Temple. The king also gave Ezra full authority to correct any abuses that had crept in among the people. When Ezra left Babylon, he had convinced six thousand Jews to return with him to Jerusalem, leading them on the journey.

They traveled four months before they reached the Holy City. When they arrived, Ezra found that even the devout Jews had gradually grown lukewarm in the practice of their religion. They had also taken wives from among the nations surrounding them, and they were in danger of falling into idolatry.

Ezra appointed two priests and two Levites to find out which of the Jews had married women who worshipped other gods. Men who had married such women were ordered to send the wives and their children away. If they refused to do so, they weren't allowed to associate with the faithful Jews.

Ezra immediately saw that the people needed instruction in their religion. So he went about building synagogues in the cities where the Jews lived. He gave orders that the people were to meet in these synagogues and listen to the Levites read the Scriptures. In this way, he brought the Sacred Scriptures back to the people.

Ezra worked hard and with great enthusiasm. When he saw that his labors were successful and that religious worship had once more been established in Palestine, he returned to Babylon.

While Ezra focused on the rites of the Temple and the religious life of the people, a second Jewish leader, named Nehemiah, was also busy at work in Jerusalem. The king had given Nehemiah, who had been his personal attendant, permission to return to Jerusalem and rebuild the walls of the city. Though Ezra had returned to Babylon, he decided to accompany Nehemiah on this journey.

As soon as Nehemiah reached Jerusalem, he assigned certain sections of the walls of the city to every family of the Jews. In spite of attacks from enemies, the people succeeded in rebuilding the walls in fifty-two days.

At this time, Tobiah, an Ammonite, was using one of the rooms in the Temple, a sacred place, as a warehouse for his personal possessions. Nehemiah threw out all of Tobiah's goods, and put in their place the vessels of the Lord that belonged there.

Tobiah was angry at Nehemiah for doing this. So he and his friends sent word to Artaxerxes, the king, that Nehemiah was planning a revolt. Nehemiah was called back by the king and questioned, but the king determined that the accusers had lied. He found Nehemiah to be innocent and loyal, and Nehemiah was allowed to return to Jerusalem.

Nehemiah continued the work of reform and worked harder than ever. He urged the rich to forgive the debts of the poor, and advised them not to demand the rents that were due. He gave them an example by not accepting the gifts from the poor that were due him as governor.

Nehemiah made arrangements for the support of the priests and Levites, and ordered that the sacrifices be offered regularly. He also insisted on the proper observance of the Sabbath.

Once back in Jerusalem, Ezra and Nehemiah refocused the people's attention on the Lord. The joy of returning home could easily have led them to lose sight of God. But these two men would not let that happen. With their minds focused on God, the people could remain faithful to Him as they came to the last days of their kingdom.

CHAPTER 22

The Last Days of the Kingdom of Judah

The Jews Are Ruled by the Greeks

For years after the time of Nehemiah, the great Persian Empire spanned three continents: from the borders of Greece in Europe to western India in Asia, and down into Egypt in Africa. Egypt, Cyprus, Phoenicia and the Greek cities of Asia Minor strove for independence, but all in vain.

In the land of Judah, trouble arose between those Jews who were faithful to the Law and to the observances of their fathers, and those who were careless. The faithful Jews kept the commandments and worshiped God according to the Law of Moses. Their high priest represented the Persian governor, and his authority was respected by the Jews who practiced the true religion.

The others, however, cared nothing about the Law. They married women who weren't Jewish and went to Samaria to worship on Mount Gerizim.

Meanwhile, new developments far away from Judea—as the land of Judah came to be called—would eventually bring new changes and challenges to the Jewish people. Alexander III, the king of the Greek kingdom of Macedon, began to extend his rule through military conquest. The new empire created by Alexander the Great, as he is commonly called, extended from his native Macedonia in the west to India in the east, and down into Egypt as well.

In the course of his many conquests, Alexander's armies defeated the Persians, so that lands that had been controlled by Persia came under the control of the Greeks. This included Palestine, where the Jews had resettled and rebuilt. For a while, the Jews were allowed to live under their own laws and worship God according to their conscience.

Heliodorus Seeks the Temple Treasure

When Alexander died, his empire was divided into four parts, each being given to one of his generals to rule. Eventually, through a succession of leaders, Jerusalem came under the rule of a man named Seleucus IV, whose lands were called the Seleucid Empire. At that time, there was a high priest named Onias. He was a holy man who hated sin and evil. While he was in office, there was peace in Jerusalem, and the laws were well kept.

Seleucus admired Onias. He sought to cooperate with the high priest in keeping the Temple holy and preserving the beauty of the divine worship. So he paid the cost of all the Temple sacrifices out of his own revenue.

But the peace didn't last long. A man named Simon, who belonged to the tribe of Benjamin and who had been appointed an overseer in the Temple, was jealous of Onias for his relationship with the king. Simon tried to undermine the influence of Onias. He approached the governor of the province and informed him that there were large sums of money in the treasury at Jerusalem. He told him that this money wasn't necessary for the sacrifices, and that it might be possible to turn it all over to the king.

The governor immediately notified Seleucus. The king's greed was stirred up; he wanted this treasure for himself. So he sent one of his officers, a man named Heliodorus, to bring it to him.

Pretending that he was on an official visit to the cities of the provinces, Heliodorus set out for Jerusalem. The high priest received him with great courtesy, but then discovered the true purpose of his mission.

Heliodorus demanded to know about the treasure. Onias said it was true that there were indeed great treasures of gold and silver laid up in the Temple. But some of these belonged to widows and orphans, and some to a man named Hyrcanus, who had left them there for safekeeping. The treasures were stored in the Temple, but they didn't belong to the Temple. So the high priest could not turn them over to the king's officer.

Heliodorus insisted that the treasure be handed over to him. He declared that he had been ordered by the king to seize the money, and he went to the Temple to find it.

No sooner had Heliodorus entered the Temple than a heavenly soldier, dressed in golden armor and seated on a horse, appeared to him. The soldier was accompanied by two other young men, beautiful and strong and glorious in appearance. The horse rushed on Heliodorus and, striking him with its front hooves, knocked him to the ground. Then the two young men stood on either side of the fallen man and whipped him furiously.

Heliodorus was carried from the Temple half-dead and terrified with fright. His companions thought he was dying and begged Onias to ask God for his recovery. Fearing that the king might think the Jews were responsible for what had happened to Heliodorus, Onias offered a sacrifice for him.

While Onias was praying, the heavenly messengers again stood before Heliodorus and said, "Be very grateful to Onias the high priest, since for his sake the Lord has granted you your life. And see that you, who have been scourged by heaven, report to all men the majestic power of God."

Then, as quickly as they had appeared, the heavenly visions vanished.

Heliodorus recovered and offered sacrifice to God. He thanked Onias for his prayers and, taking his troops with him, returned to the king.

Antiochus Persecutes the Jews
Years passed, and Antiochus Epiphanes became king of the Seleucid Empire. Returning from his failed military campaigns against Egypt, he stormed Jerusalem. He took as prisoners thousands of the inhabitants, and he sold them as slaves. Many thousands more he killed, including women and children.

To show his contempt for the Jewish religion, Antiochus entered the Temple, removed the sacred vessels, and plundered the treasury. Then he offered unclean animals on the altar.

Antiochus was determined to break down the loyalty of the Jews to their nation and to their religion. Two years after his first attack on the city, he returned and took possession of it. He destroyed the houses and the walls, and he made a fort for his troops on Mount Zion.

Antiochus forbade the Jews to offer sacrifices to their God. He tried to force them to worship the gods of the Greeks instead. The Temple of the true God was made the temple of false gods, and pagans went to the

Temple to worship their idols and offer unclean animals on the altar. In all the cities of Judah, pagan altars were set up and pagan worship was required. Anyone who followed the laws of the Jews and who observed the Sabbath was punished by death.

Once a month a search was completed for copies of the books of the Law, and those who had them in their possession were put to death. Great numbers of the Jews fled from the cities to avoid this persecution, while others were sold into slavery.

These persecutions were brutal, and many Jews followed the new pagan laws to escape trouble. But those who remained faithful were only made stronger. They became more devoted to the customs of Israel and to the worship of the true God. Their heroism was so great that many suffered martyrdom, persevering in their loyalty even to death.

The Martyrdom of Eleazar

Eleazar, ninety years old, was one of the important men of the nation. He was brought before the governor and accused of keeping the commandments of the Jewish law. The governor commanded him to eat pork, knowing it was against the Law of Moses. Eleazar bravely refused, because this act was forbidden by God.

His friends begged him to obey the king to save his life. But he refused to follow their advice.

Next, they urged him just to eat some other kind of meat and pretend that it was pork. But Eleazar would not deceive the king, even to save his life. Besides, he explained, men can deceive their kings, but they cannot deceive God. He thought, too, of the good example he might set for the youth of his nation if he were to stand up to the oppressors of his people.

The aged man aroused the pity and respect of some who were standing by. But Eleazar was eventually led to the pillar of scourging and beaten to death. He died a martyr, faithful and obedient to God.

The Family of Martyrs
Eleazar was not alone among the Jewish martyrs. Seven brothers, together with their mother, were brought before King Antiochus and accused of disobedience to his law. They were ordered to eat pork. But like Eleazar, they refused.

The oldest brother said, "We are ready to die rather than transgress the laws of our fathers."

When the king heard this, he was enraged. He ordered huge pans and bronze kettles to be made hot. They cut out the tongue of the brother who had spoken out courageously against the king, and his scalp was torn off. They also chopped off his hands and feet. His mother and his brothers were forced to watch this cruel scene.

Finally, while he was still alive, he was brought to the fire to be fried in the pan, as if he were a piece of food. His sufferings were terrible, but all the while his mother and brothers urged him to maintain his courage and stand fast.

After the first brother was dead, they took the second and, having torn off his scalp as well, they asked him: "Will you eat rather than have your body punished limb by limb?"

"No," came his simple reply.

So they forced him to bear the same horrible torments that his older brother had endured. But with his dying breath he said to the king, "You accursed wretch, you dismiss us from this present life, but the King of the universe will raise us up to an everlasting renewal of life, because we have died for His laws."

The third brother followed him to death, as did the fourth and the fifth and the sixth. Their noble mother stood by and watched them in their sufferings, urging them to be brave and to refuse the king's demands.

At last, only the youngest boy was left. The king, seeing that all his cruelty was having no effect, attempted to win the boy away from God by kind words. He promised him that he would make him a rich and happy man, that he would take him for his friend and give him everything he wanted in this life, if he would only turn away from the laws of his fathers.

When the boy refused to listen to him, the king called his mother over and told her to advise her son not to be stubborn and to obey the commands of the king.

But she scoffed at the cruel tyrant. Turning to her boy, she said: "I do not know how you came into being in my womb. It was not I who gave you life and breath, nor I who set in order the elements within each of you. Therefore the Creator of the world, who shaped the beginning of man and devised the origin of all things, will in his mercy give life and breath back to you again, since you now forget yourselves for the sake of his laws. . . . Do not fear this butcher, but prove worthy of your brothers. Accept death, so that in God's mercy I may get you back again with your brothers."

Then the brave boy said, "I will not obey the king's command, but I obey the command of the law that was given to our fathers through Moses." Then turning to the king, he said, "But you, who have contrived all sorts of evil against the Hebrews, will certainly not escape the hands of God."

When the king heard this, he became even more furious. He ordered the youngest son and the mother to be tortured even more cruelly than the others. Both died bravely, giving glory to God and refusing to sin against His law.

As we've noted, many events in the Old Testament foreshadow events in the New Testament. Doesn't the mother of the seven brothers remind us of Mary, the Mother of God, who was forced to watch her own son suffer? Other brave believers in the New Testament will also show us what it's like to suffer for their faith.

But the martyrdom of God's people didn't end with the people who lived in biblical times. In every age down to the present, people of good faith and courage have been persecuted and even put to death. Not only long ago, but today as well, the Church has countless martyrs in her ranks. Like Eleazar, they stand up for what is right and stand strong with God.

Notice too how the Jews who persevered through these persecutions were strengthened in their faith. Yet when they enjoyed times of prosperity, many of them abandoned their religion, customs, and laws. They forgot about the God they needed when life was filled with blessings, and they returned to Him only in their times of greatest need.

We must ask ourselves: Do we also forget about God when things are going well, and return to Him only in times of need?

In the face of persecution, we should note that not all the Jews who stood up to their oppressors ended up as martyrs. Instead, some took up the sword to drive away God's enemies.

Mattathias and His Sons Resist Antiochus
Among the families who fled from Jerusalem during the days of the persecution of Antiochus was the family of Mattathias. He had five sons: John, Simon, Judas

Maccabeus, Eleazar, and Jonathan. With them, he escaped to the nearby mountains to join others in hiding.

Antiochus sent his army in search of the fugitives. When the troops found them, they tried to force the refugees to submit to the king's commands. Many of them yielded and offered sacrifice to the idols. But Mattathias and his sons refused to offer sacrifice to any but the true God.

Mattathias and his sons escaped again and fled again to the mountains. They came to be known as the *Maccabees,* and a large group of fighting men, passionate about their faith, gathered around them. With the help of these men, Mattathias attacked various towns, drove out the forces of Antiochus, and punished the Jews who had surrendered to the king.

After a year of this type of warfare, Mattathias died. He gave the command of his army to his son, Judas Maccabeus.

Judas continued the warfare begun by his father. Though his army was small, he conquered the generals of Antiochus in four battles. After the fourth victory, the Jews enjoyed peace for a while.

The victorious Jews began at once to purify the Temple, which had been used for pagan sacrifices. They consecrated a new altar of sacrifice by offering animals on it for eight days. This event would be commemorated every year afterward.

Now a number of the Jews had fled to the territory of neighboring nations for protection. But they weren't welcome in these distant lands, and these nations began to persecute them. Mattathias's son Judas came to their rescue. He defeated the Edomites, Ammonites, and Philistines, and brought the refugees back to Jerusalem.

After one of the battles with the Edomites, Judas discovered that some of his soldiers who had been killed in battle had carried under their clothing a token of pagan idols. These tokens had been forbidden by the Law, because they were used in worshiping false gods. Judas concluded that the men had been slain for their disobedience.

Even so, Judas knew that they had been good and brave soldiers, and that they had sinned through human weakness. So he ordered a large sum of money to be sent to Jerusalem. It was to be used for a sacrifice, with prayers, to be offered for the sins of the dead.

As the inspired biblical author tells us, this intention of Judas was "a holy and pious thought." By sacrifice and prayer, "he made atonement for the dead, that they might be delivered from their sin."

We should note an important element of this story. When Judas Maccabeus had prayers and sacrifices offered for the dead, he showed us that we can do the same. Today, to help our departed loved ones, we can pray for them and have the holy sacrifice of the Mass offered for them.

Now Antiochus was in Persia when he heard that his army had been defeated by Judas Maccabeus. At that same time, he himself had just been defeated in battle by an enemy king. In his shame, he determined to take revenge on the Jews, so he started for Jerusalem.

But on the way he was stricken with a terrible disease. He was in great pain, yet he tried to go on. He continued on the journey until he fell from his chariot and could go no farther.

The flesh fell from his bones, and the stench from his body was so great that no one could bear to be near him. He cried out to God for mercy and promised to give independence to the Jews. But his repentance was not sincere, and God did not answer his prayer. Antiochus died a miserable death in the mountains of a strange country.

The Last Campaigns of Judas Maccabeus

Judas Maccabeus next attacked the Syrian fortress atop Mount Zion. During the siege, some Syrian soldiers escaped from the fortress. They, along with traitors from the Jewish army, went to Antiochus Eupator, who was then king of Syria, to ask for help.

The king marched on Jerusalem with a large army. Judas left the ongoing battle on Mount Zion and marched to meet him, placing his army near a mountain pass where he could meet the companies of the enemy's army one at a time.

A fierce battle followed. Judas saw that the king's army was too powerful for him. He retreated to Jerusalem, and Antiochus Eupator followed, making plans to attack the Temple.

The army of Judas Maccabeus had little food to sustain them. He would have been compelled to surrender, but as it turned out, other battles in the Syrian state made it necessary for Antiochus to refocus his forces and attention. So he returned to Antioch.

But this was only a short break for Judas Maccabeus and his men. Antiochus Eupator later sent two armies to Palestine, the second of which was led by a man named Nicanor. Judas tried to drive Nicanor's forces out of the country, but at this point he had only three thousand men in his army. The situation looked bleak for Judas and his men.

But before the battle, Judas had a vision in which Onias, the high priest, and Jeremiah, the prophet, appeared to him and promised victory. With confidence, he led his men into battle. The vision came true, as

Judas and his men won the battle. Thirty-five thousand Syrian soldiers were killed, and Nicanor was captured and executed.

At this time, Judas Maccabeus thought of making an alliance with Rome, a growing power that was opposed to the Greeks and Syrians. He sent ambassadors to Rome, where they were received warmly.

In the agreement that was made between Rome and Judas, the Jews promised to help the Romans in war, and the Romans promised to protect the Jews. As a result of this alliance, the Romans sent word to Demetrius, the Syrian, warning him not to mistreat the Jews any longer, or he would have the Roman legions to contend with.

But while the ambassadors were still in Rome, a third army marched from Syria against Judas. He was camped at Laisa with only three thousand men, most of whom fled when they saw the great numbers of their enemy. Judas was grossly outmatched as he went to battle with only eight hundred men. He was eventually killed, leaving Jonathan, his younger brother, to take up his post at the head of the Jewish army.

Though the Syrians had some success, they had become weary of trying to conquer the Jews. When the ambassadors from Rome finally arrived to announce the treaty between the Jewish nation and Rome, the Syrians recalled their army.

Shortly after this, Jonathan was murdered. He was succeeded by Simon, whose reign was peaceful for many years.

After the time of the Maccabees, the rulers of the Jewish people were engaged in civil war for about five years. Brother rose up against brother, and chaos ensued. Amid the turmoil, the Roman emperor appointed a foreigner, an Edomite whose name was Herod, to step in and re-store order by becoming the king of Judah.

In this way, the time had come at last that had been foretold by Jacob on his deathbed. Though the scepter had passed from Judah, a new and glorious scepter would arise from among his descendants—the Savior for whom the world was waiting.

THE BOOKS OF THE OLD TESTAMENT

Genesis
Exodus
Leviticus
Numbers
Deuteronomy
Joshua
Judges
Ruth
1 Samuel
2 Samuel
1 Kings
2 Kings
1 Chronicles
2 Chronicles
Ezra
Nehemiah
Tobit
Judith
Esther
Job
Psalms
Proverbs
Ecclesiastes
Song of Solomon (Song of Songs)

Wisdom
Sirach
Isaiah
Jeremiah
Lamentations
Baruch
Ezekiel
Daniel
Hosea
Joel
Amos
Obadiah
Jonah
Micah
Nahum
Habakkuk
Zephaniah
Haggai
Zechariah
Malachi
1 Maccabees
2 Maccabees

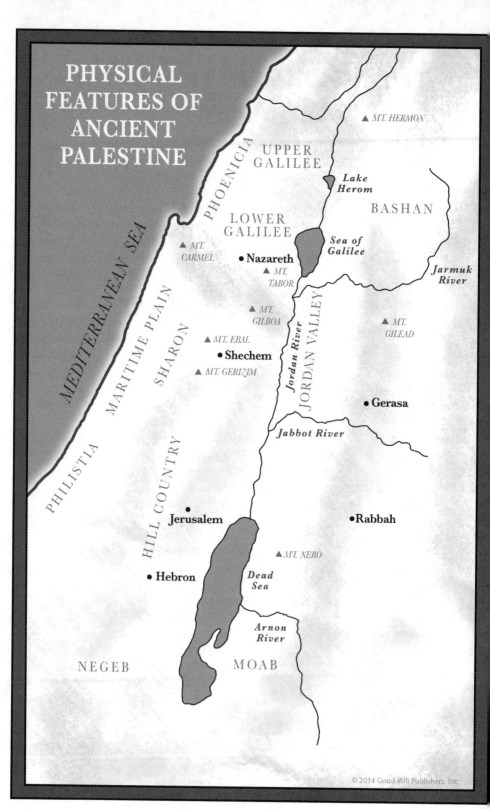

PHYSICAL FEATURES OF ANCIENT PALESTINE

▲ MT. HERMON

PHOENICIA

UPPER GALILEE

Lake Herom

BASHAN

LOWER GALILEE

MEDITERRANEAN SEA

▲ MT. CARMEL

• Nazareth

Sea of Galilee

▲ MT. TABOR

Jarmuk River

▲ MT. GILBOA

Jordan River

▲ MT. GILEAD

MARITIME PLAIN

SHARON

▲ MT. EBAL

• Shechem

▲ MT. GERIZIM

JORDAN VALLEY

• Gerasa

Jabbot River

PHILISTIA

HILL COUNTRY

• Jerusalem

•Rabbah

▲ MT. NEBO

• Hebron

Dead Sea

Arnon River

NEGEB

MOAB

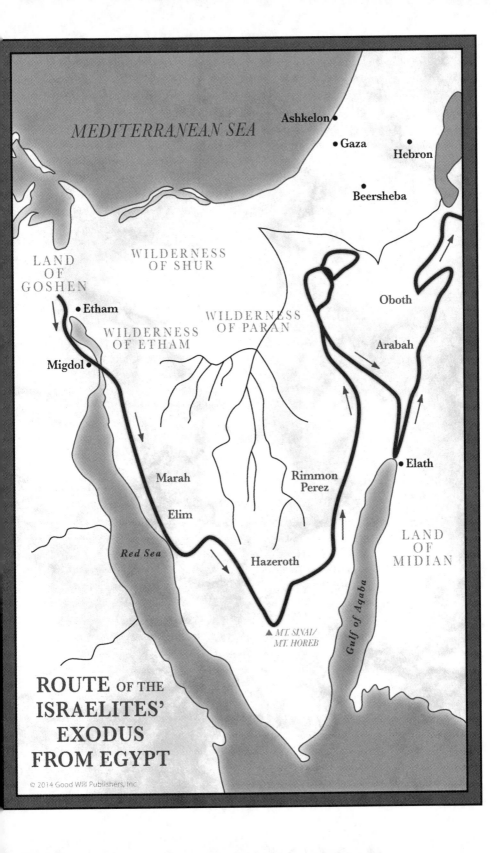

MEDITERRANEAN SEA

Ashkelon•
• Gaza
Hebron

• Beersheba

WILDERNESS
OF SHUR

LAND
OF
GOSHEN

Oboth

• Etham

WILDERNESS
OF PARAN

WILDERNESS
OF ETHAM

Arabah

Migdol•

Marah

Rimmon
Perez

• Elath

Elim

Red Sea

LAND
OF
MIDIAN

Hazeroth

Gulf of Aqaba

▲ MT. SINAI/
MT. HOREB

ROUTE OF THE
ISRAELITES'
EXODUS
FROM EGYPT

© 2014 Good Will Publishers, Inc

CANAAN'S EARLY INHABITANTS

HIVITES

HITTITES

Lake Herom

GERGESENES

Sea of Galilee

MEDITERRANEAN SEA

CANAANITES

PERIZZITES

HIVITES

CANAANITES

Jordan River

AMORITES

PHILISTINES

JEBUSITES

HITTITES

AMORITES

Dead Sea

MOABITES

EDOMITES

© 2014 Good Will Publishers, Inc

THE DIVIDED
KINGDOM OF
ISRAEL
AND JUDAH

• Damascus

• Sidon

PHOENICIA

Tyre •   Dan •

KINGDOM OF
DAMASCUS

Sea of
Galilee

MEDITERRANEAN SEA

Samaria
•

ISRAEL

• Joppa

Bethel
•

Jordan River

AMMON

Gaza
•

PHILISTIA

Jerusalem
•

Dead
Sea

• Beersheba

MOAB

JUDAH

King's Highway

EGYPT

• Kadesh Barnea

JUDAH

EDOM

Elat •
• Ezion Geber

EGYPT

© 2014 Good Will Publishers, Inc

INDEX

Aaron, 75–81, 90, 109. *See also*
  Moses
Abel (son of Adam and Eve),
  19–22
Abiram, 111
Abraham, 29–34; death of, 42; as
  "father in faith," 40; God
  tests, 35–41; and Lot,
  29–32; loyalty of, 40; and
  Melchizedek, 32; sons
  of (*see* Isaac; Ishmael); in
  valley of Mamre, 31–32
Abram (son of Terah). *See*
  Abraham
Absalom (son of David), 168–70
Adam, 14–18; and the Blessed
  Virgin Mary, 17; clothes
  of, 17; and the Devil,
  16–17; disobedience of, 18;
  and the forbidden fruit,
  16–17; and the Lord
  Jesus Christ, 18; original
  righteousness of, 18.
  See also Eve
Ahab: campaign against king of
  Syria, 198; death of, 199;
  and death of Naboth,
  198–99; Elijah meeting

with, 194–96; and Jezebel,
  198–99
Altar, types of, 100
Amorites, 113–14, 123
Angels, 8–9
Ark of Covenant, 99, 166–68
Arnon (river), 120, 123
Asa (son of Abijam), 190
Asenath (wife of Joseph), 60
Asher (son of Jacob), 50
Assyrians: and Hezekiah (king
  of Judah), 216–18; invade
  Israel, 212–18; Judith saves
  kingdom from, 218–20
Azymes (unleavened bread), 105

Babel, 26–28
Babylonia: attack on Jerusalem,
  221–24
Balaam, 115–17
Balak (king of the Moabites), 115
Bathsheba (wife of Uriah), 170–72
Benjamin (son of Jacob), 52, 62–65
Bethel (House of God), 30, 49
Bethlehem, 52
Book of Genesis: creation account,
  10–12; creation of man in,
  13; free will in, 13
Book of Nature, 2–3

Holocausts, 102
Holy of Holies, 99, 181
Holy Place, 180
House of God, 49
House of the Forest of Lebanon,
181

Infallibility of the Church, 5
Intellect (the ability to think), 8
Isaac (son of Abraham and Sarah),
33, 36–38; death of, 52;
marriage of, 41–42
Ishmael (son of Abraham and
Hagar), 33, 36–37
Israel. *See* Jacob (son of Isaac and
Rebecca)
Israelites, 69; and Amalekites, 90;
and Balaam, 115–17; and
desert wanderings, 107–17;
and Gideon, 133–35; and
the judges, 132–36; and the
last years of Moses,
112–15; Mount Sinai,
departing from, 107–9;
and the origin of Samson,
135–36; and the origin of
Samuel, 139–40, 147–50;
punishment of, 113–14; as
spies and rebels, 109–12;
and the story of Ruth,
143–46
Issachar (son of Jacob), 50; tribe
of, 108

Jabbok (river), 120
Jacob (son of Isaac and Rebecca),
43–52; in Bethlehem, 52;
and the blessings of Isaac,
46; children of, 50; death
of, 66; flees to Haran, 49;
marriage to Rachel, 50
Jeremiah, warnings of, 221–23
Jeroboam, 183–84; and the city of
Bethel, 187; and the city of
Dan, 187; and Josiah, 187;
and Shechem, 187
Jerusalem, 30, 32, 119–20, 127,
165–66, 168–69, 183, 184,
241–49; attack on, 221–23;
as capital, 165–66, 168;
as the City of David, 166;
and the decree of Cyrus,
241–42; Esther as queen
of, 243–44; and Ezra and
Nehemiah, 247–49; and
Haman,
244–48; and the
inhabitants of Canaan,
121–23; return to, 242–
43; temple rebuilding in,
242–43
Jesus Christ, 98; and Adam, 18
Jethro (father-in-law of Moses),
73, 91
Jews: and Antiochus, 254–55;
also known as Hebrews,
5; and Daniel, 85, 233–34;
elders of, 226; and Esther,

THE STORY OF
THE BIBLE
Hear the Bible Come Alive Like Never Before

Brilliantly read and performed, this audio dramatization will bring alive in your home or car the most beloved Biblical stories from both the Old and New Testament. Sound effects, music and voice acting complement the narration, with 15 hours of content. You will be transported back in time by simply closing your eyes!

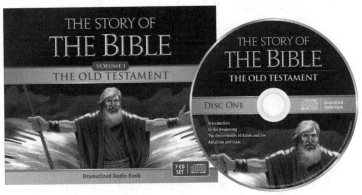

The Old Testament

978-1-61890-644-1 · 7 DISCS · 7.5 Hours · $39.95

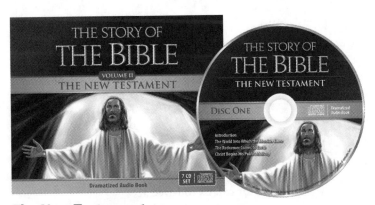

The New Testament

978-1-61890-650-2 · 7 DISCS · 7.5 Hours · $39.95

www.TANBooks.com

TAN·BOOKS

TAN Books was founded in 1967 to preserve the spiritual, intellectual and liturgical traditions of the Catholic Church. At a critical moment in history TAN kept alive the great classics of the Faith and drew many to the Church. In 2008 TAN was acquired by Saint Benedict Press. Today TAN continues its mission to a new generation of readers.

From its earliest days TAN has published a range of booklets that teach and defend the Faith. Through partnerships with organizations, apostolates, and mission-minded individuals, well over 10 million TAN booklets have been distributed.

More recently, TAN has expanded its publishing with the launch of Catholic calendars and daily planners—as well as Bibles, fiction, and multimedia products through its sister imprints Catholic Courses (CatholicCourses.com) and Saint Benedict Press (SaintBenedictPress.com). In 2015, TAN Homeschool became the latest addition to the TAN family, preserving the Faith for the next generation of Catholics (www.TANHomeschool.com).

Today TAN publishes over 500 titles in the areas of theology, prayer, devotions, doctrine, Church history, and the lives of the saints. TAN books are published in multiple languages and found throughout the world in schools, parishes, bookstores and homes.

For a free catalog, visit us online at
TANBooks.com

Or call us toll-free at
(800) 437-5876